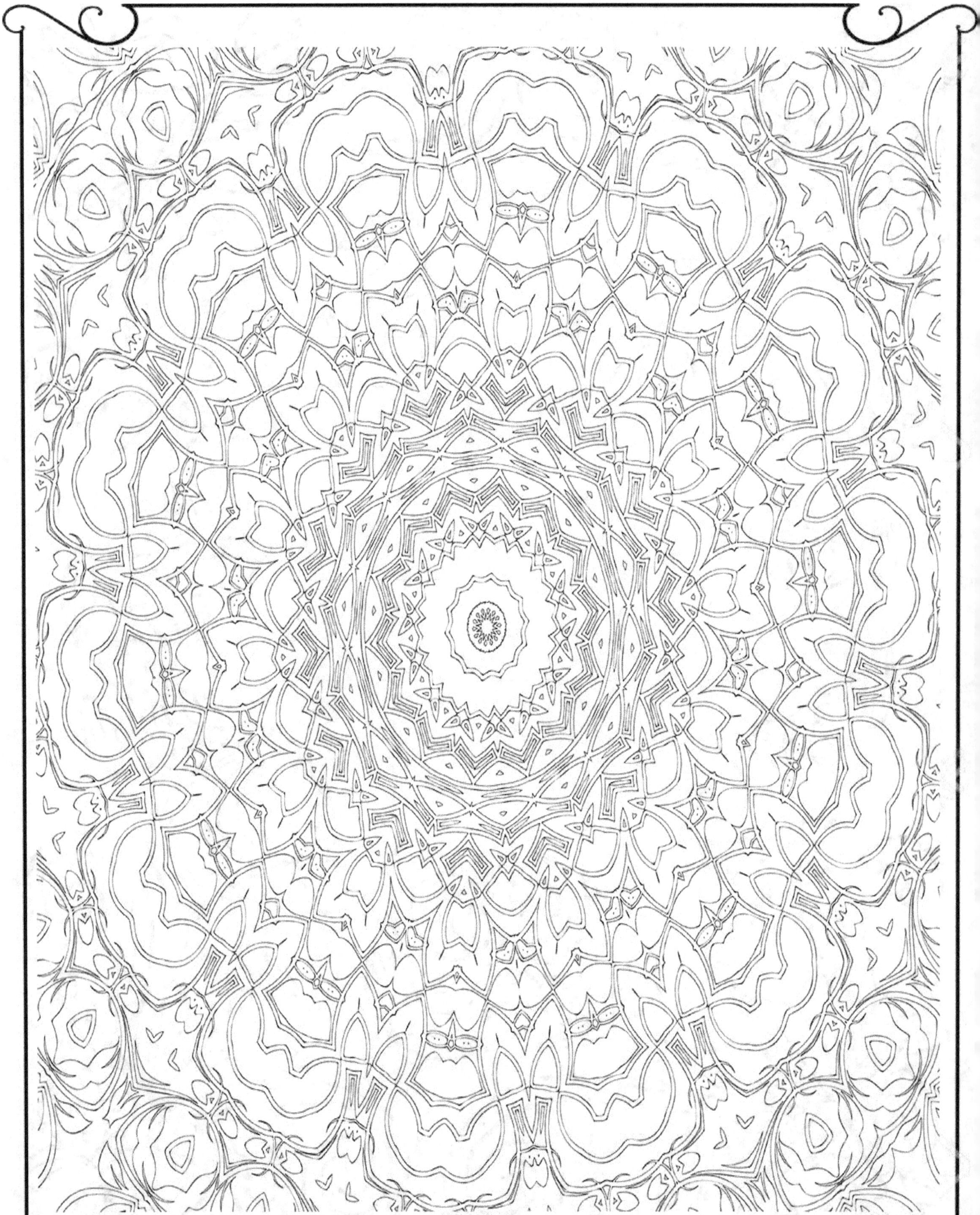

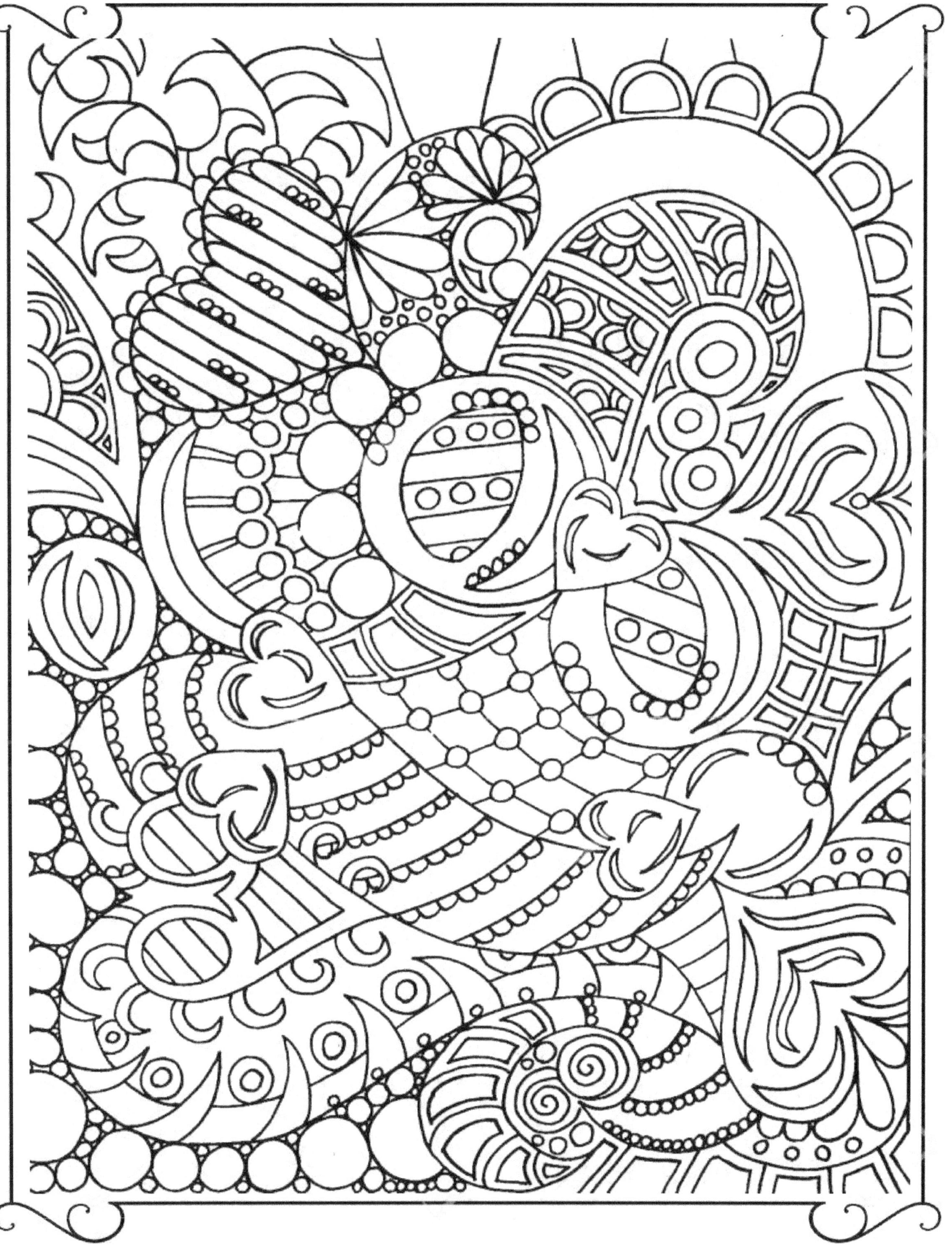

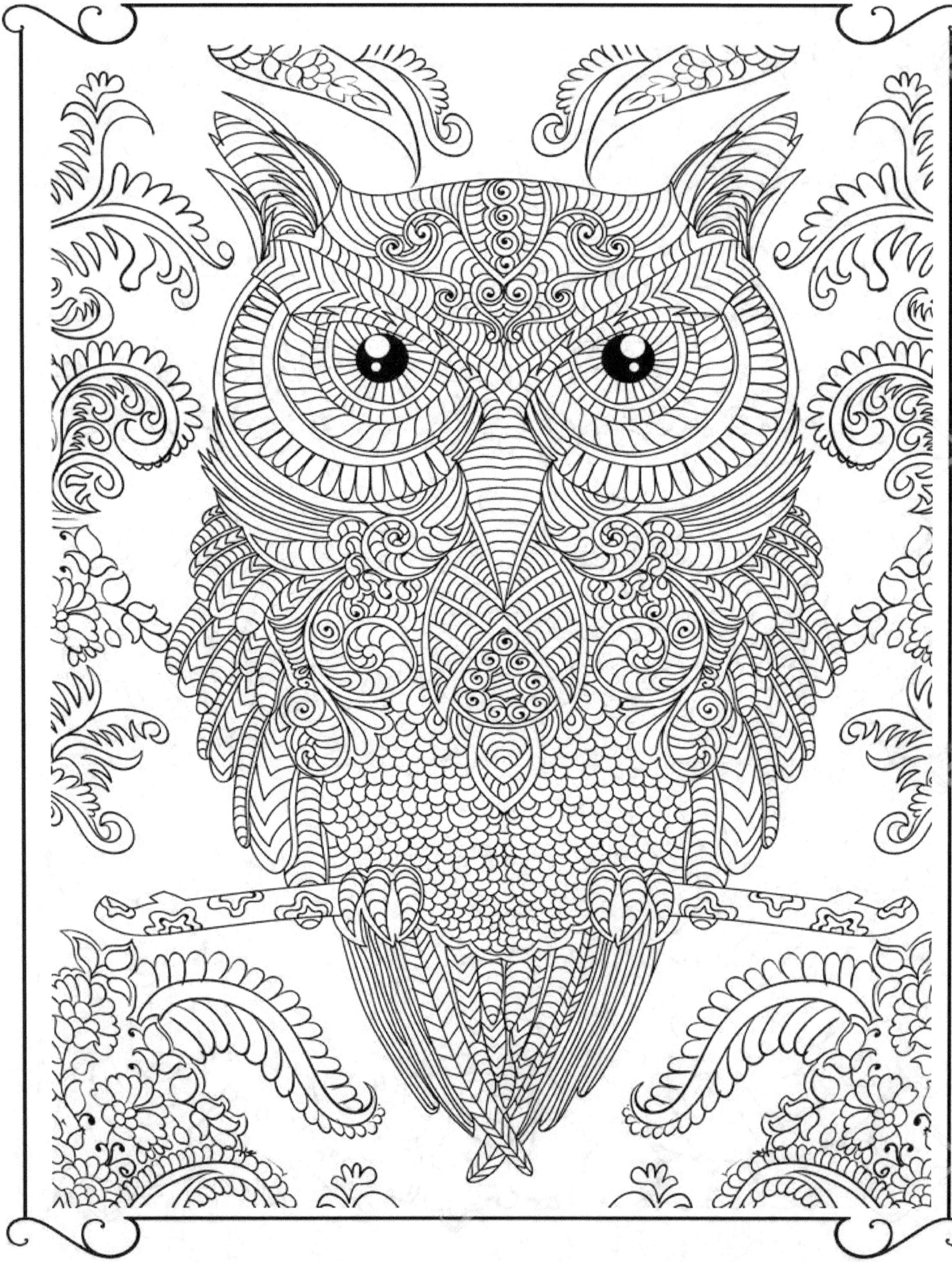

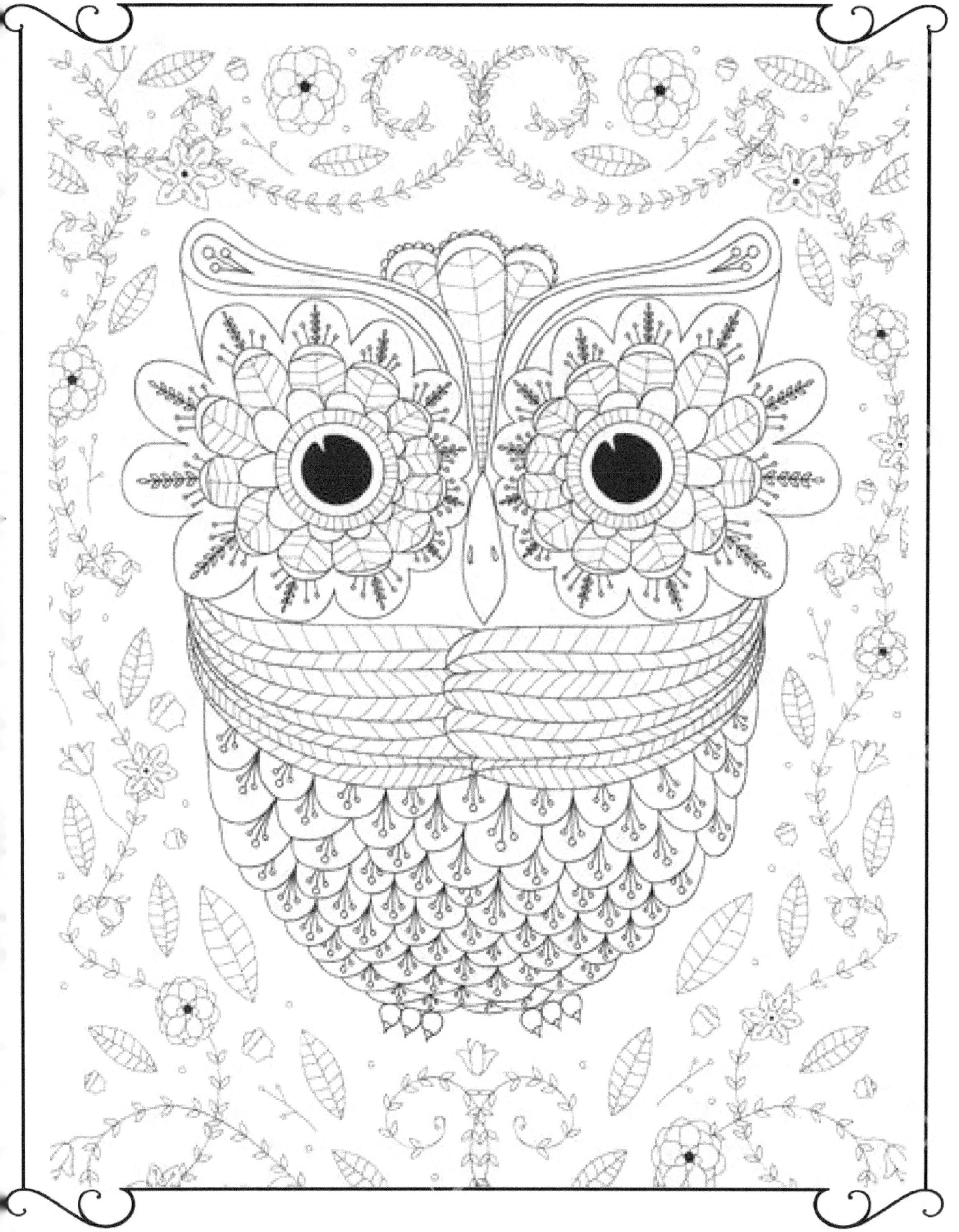

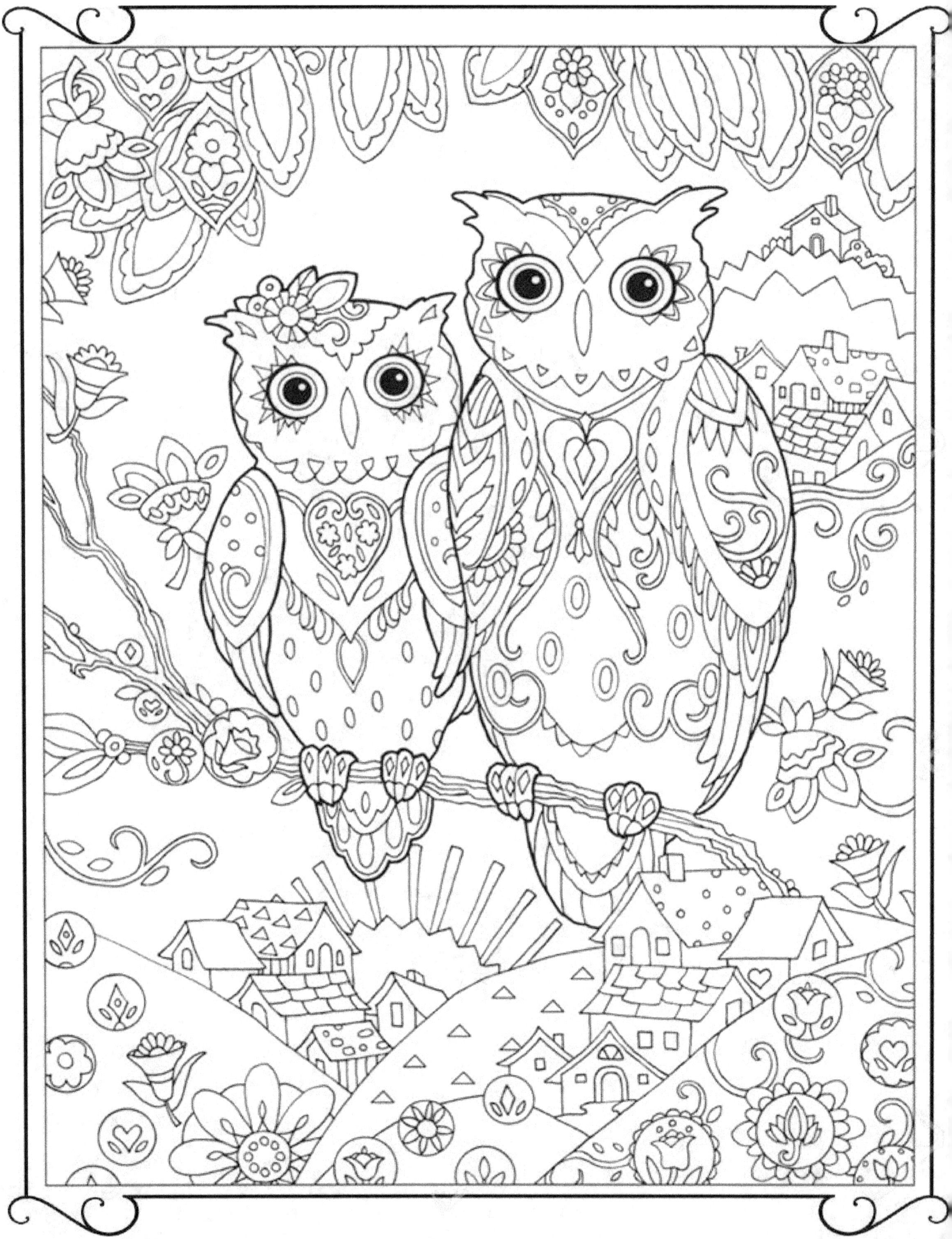

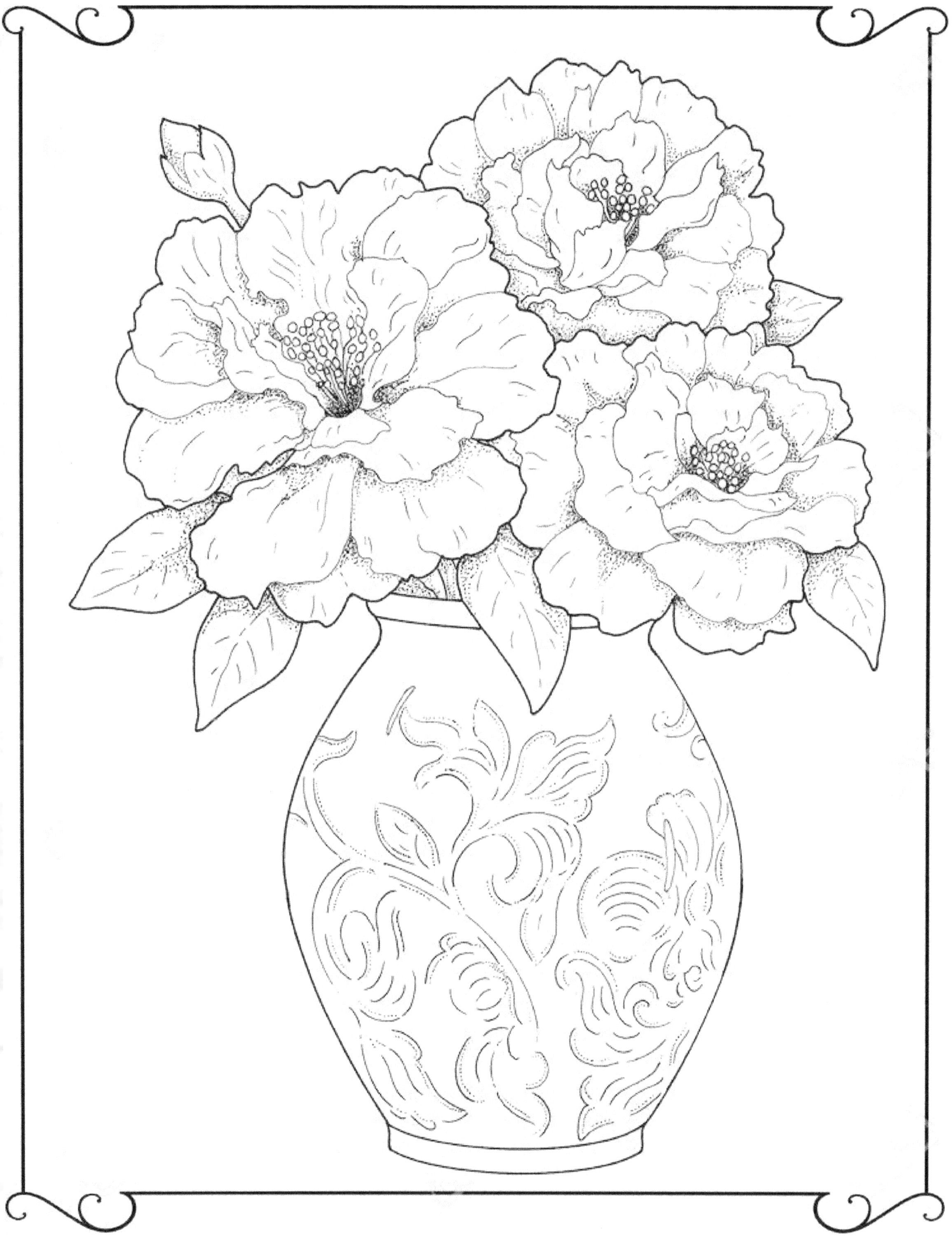

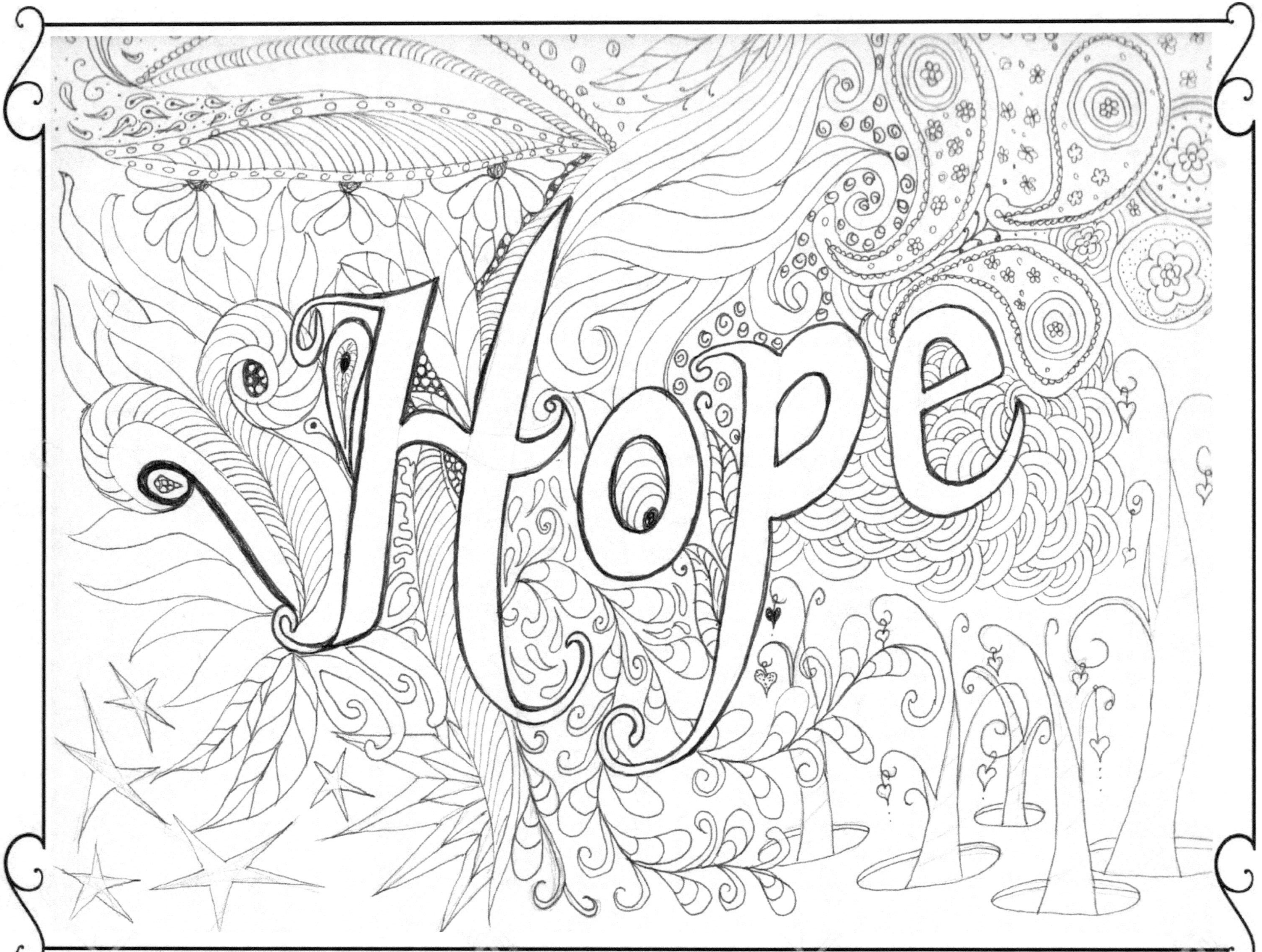
Hope

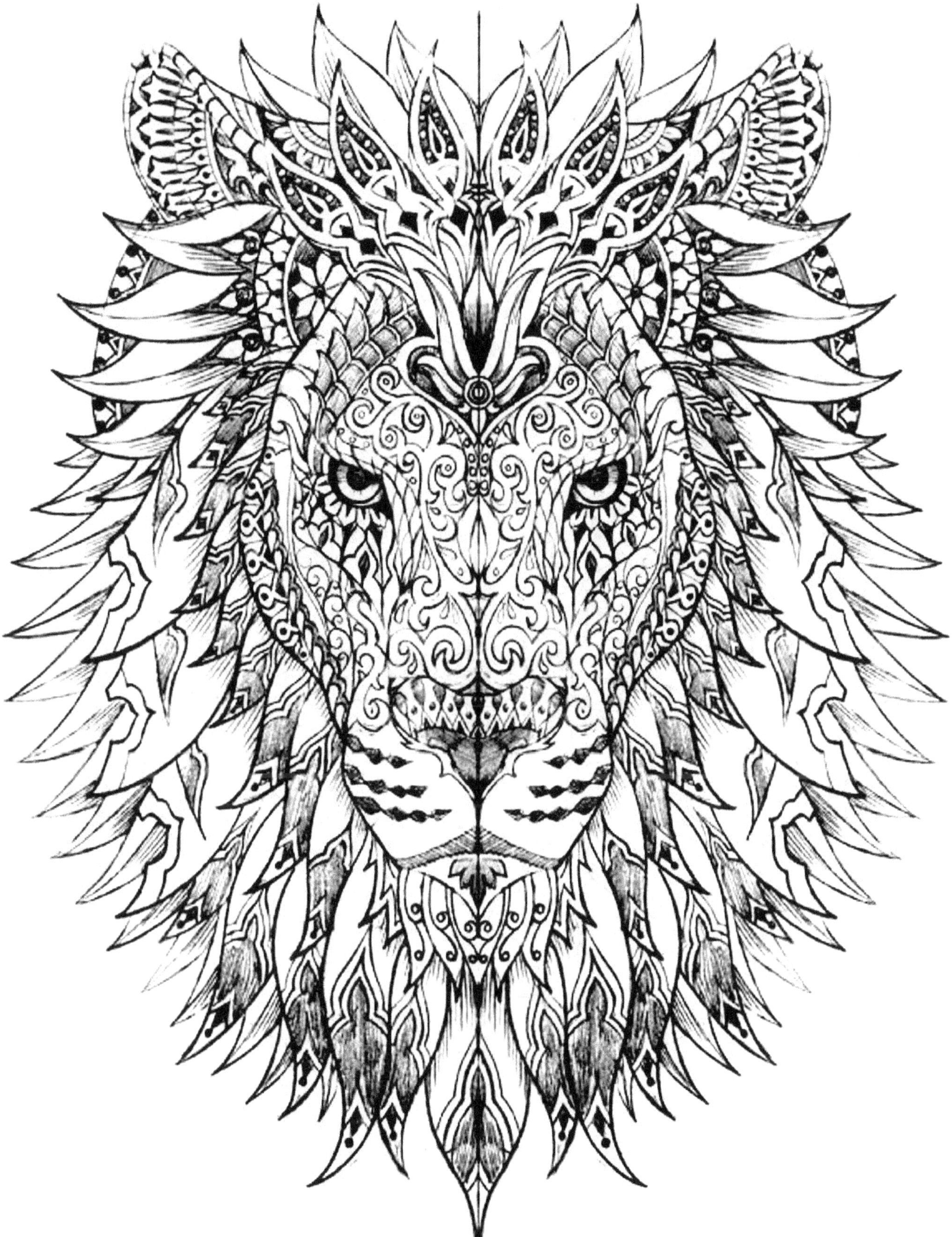

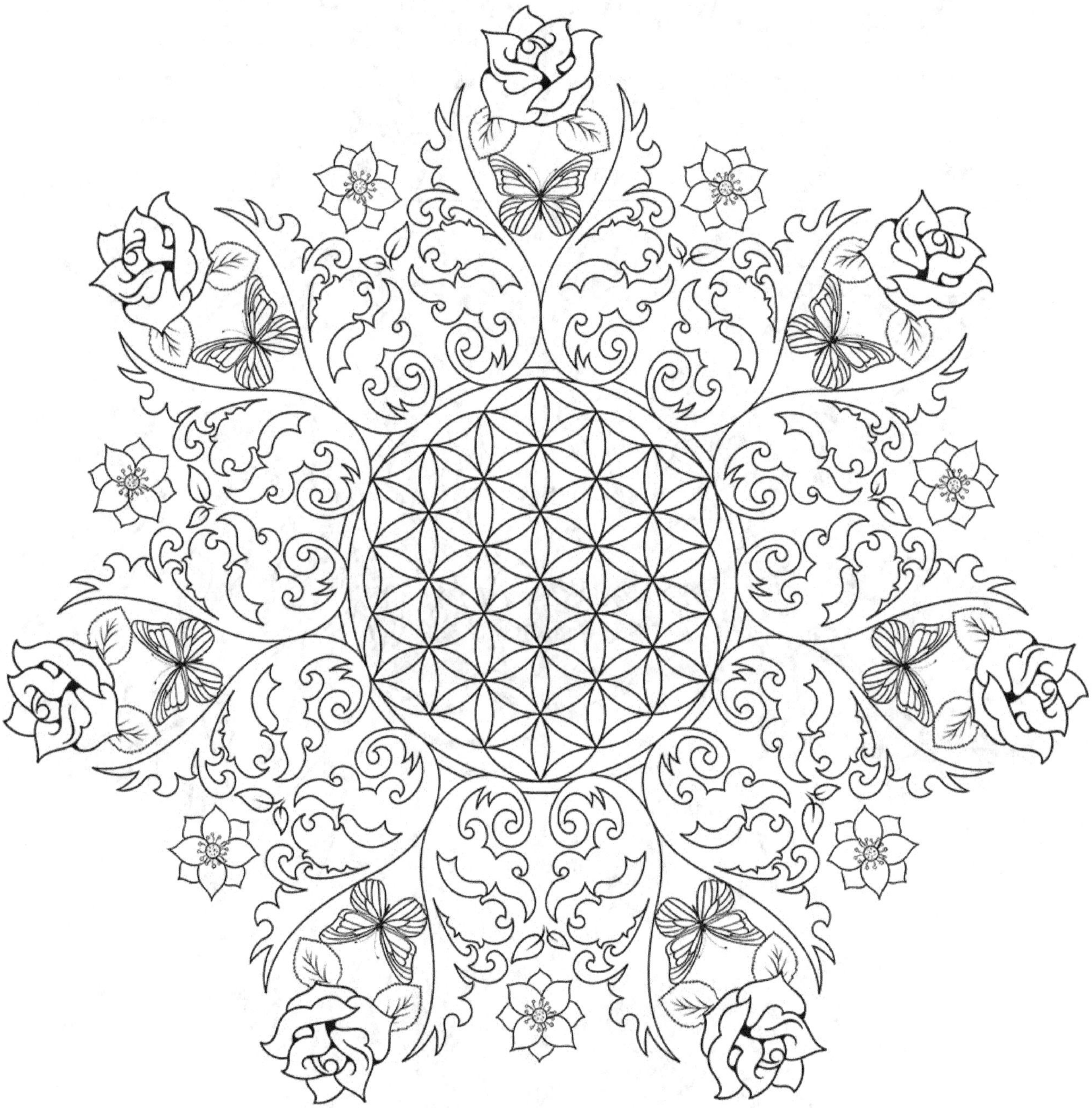

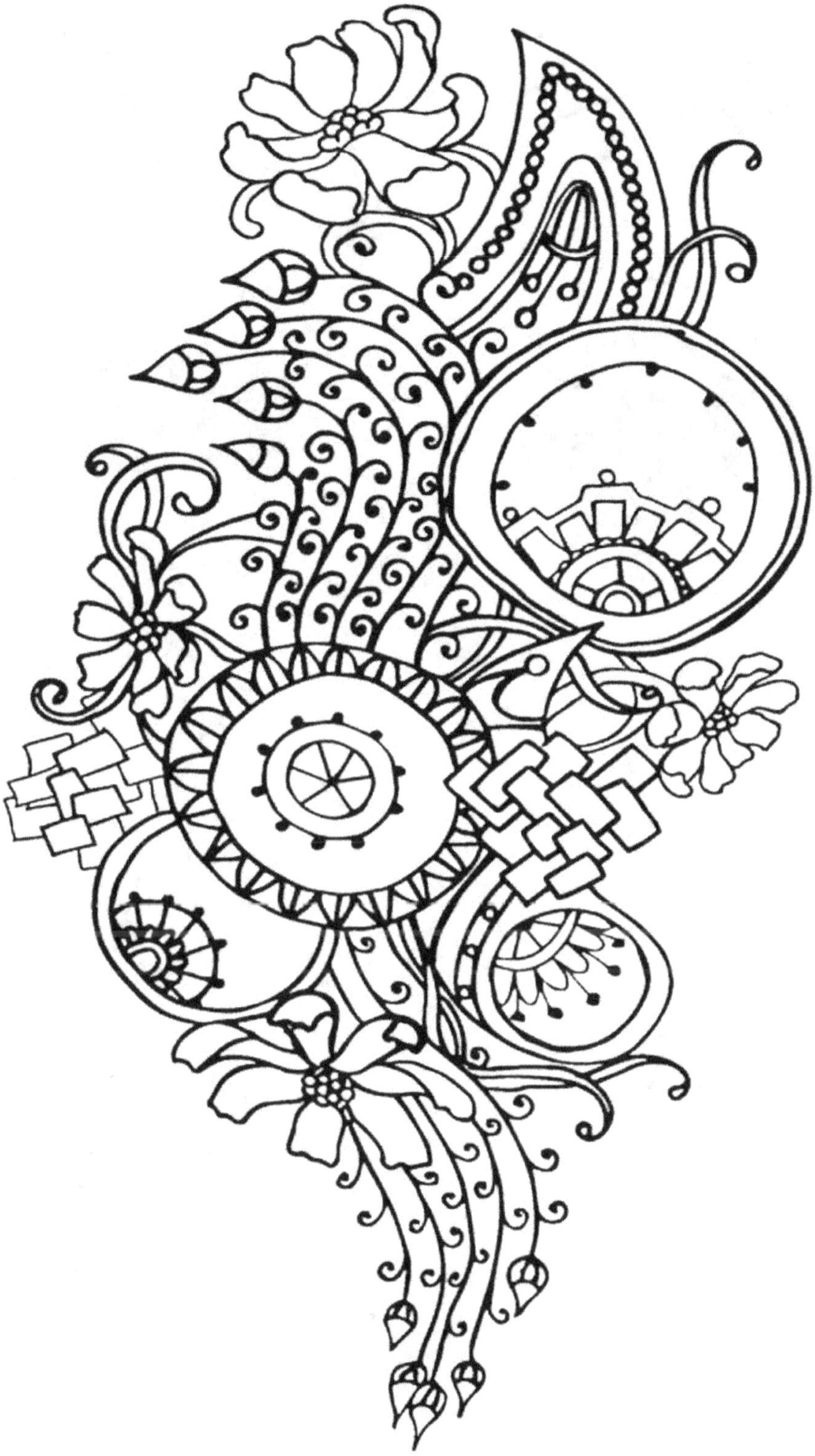

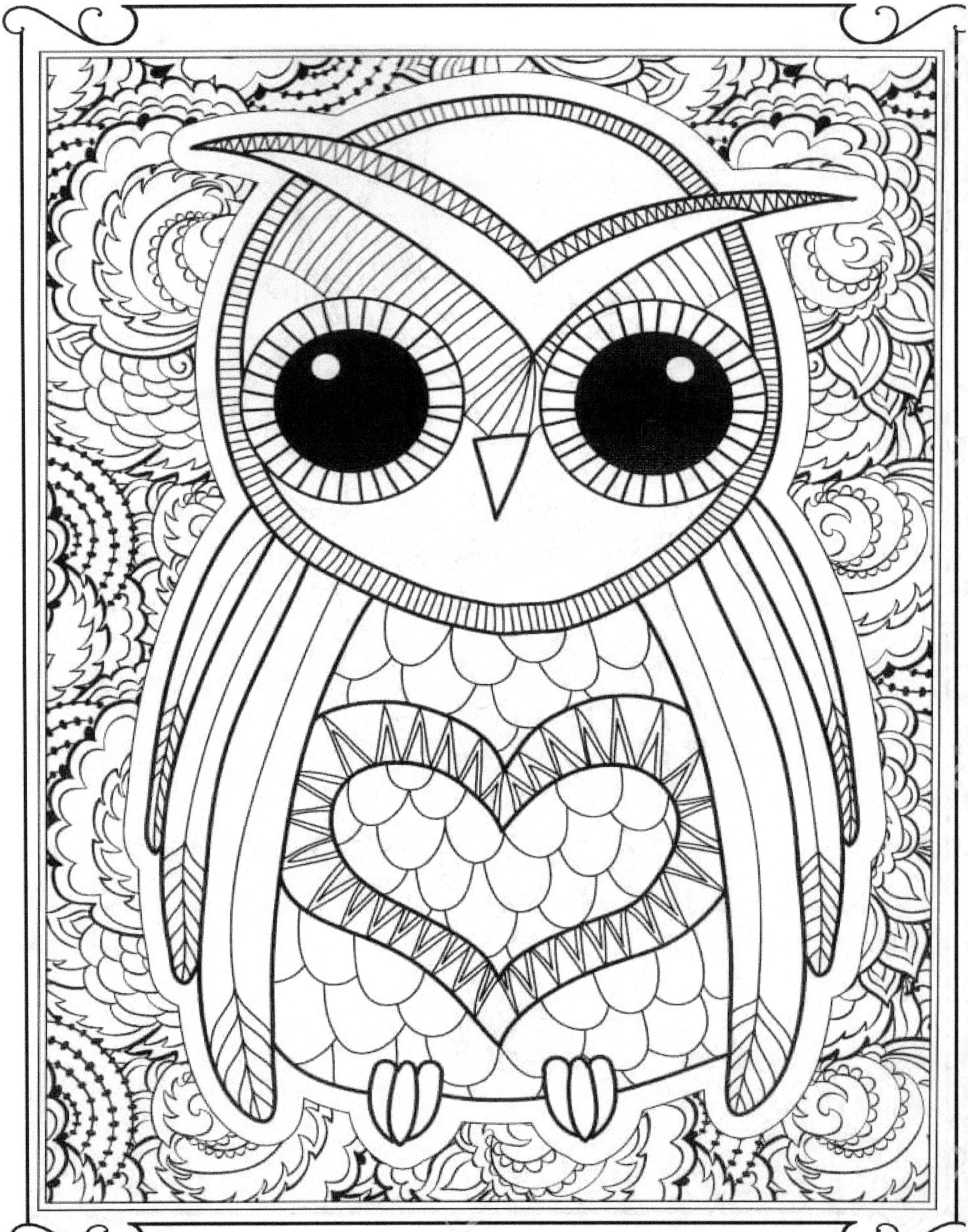

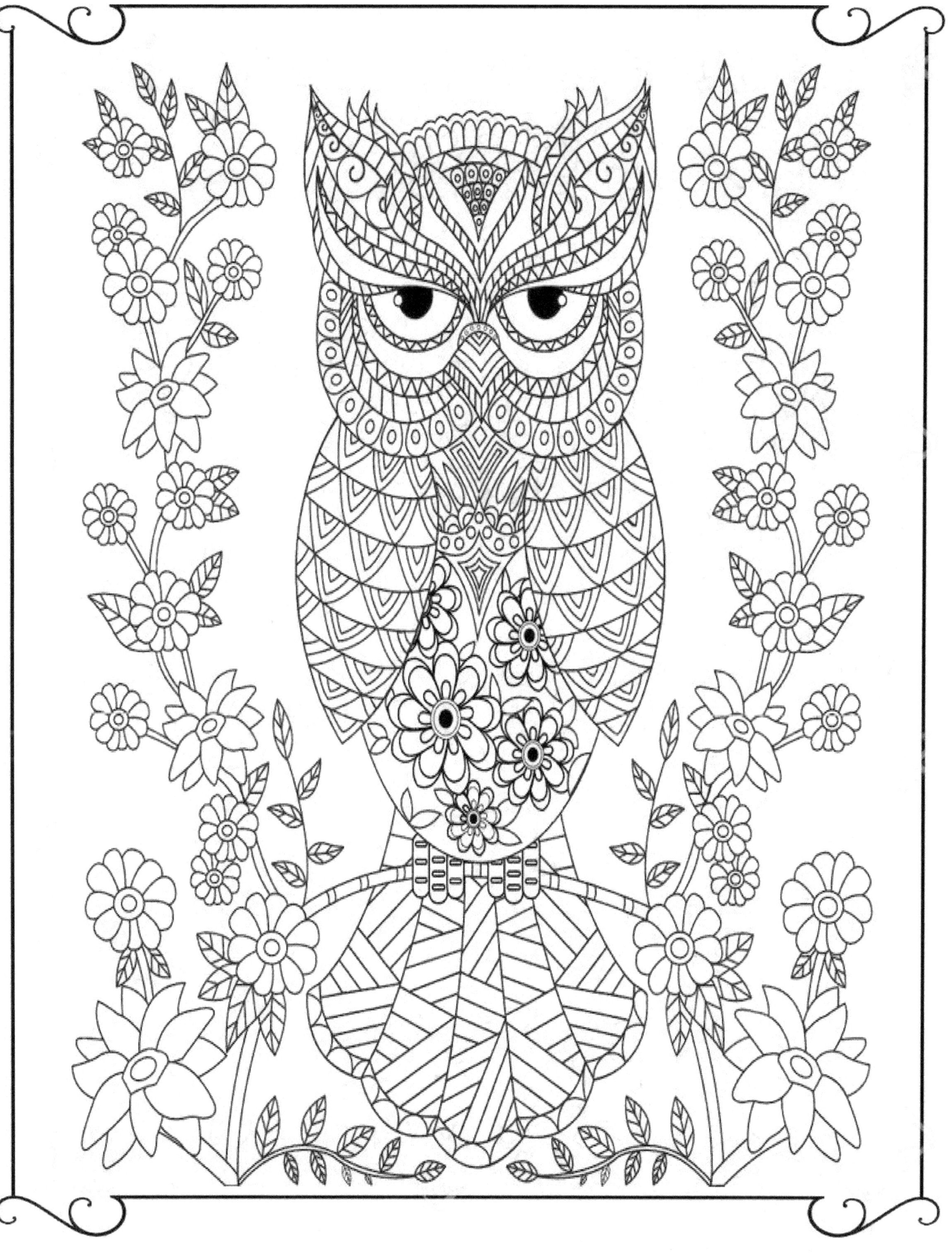

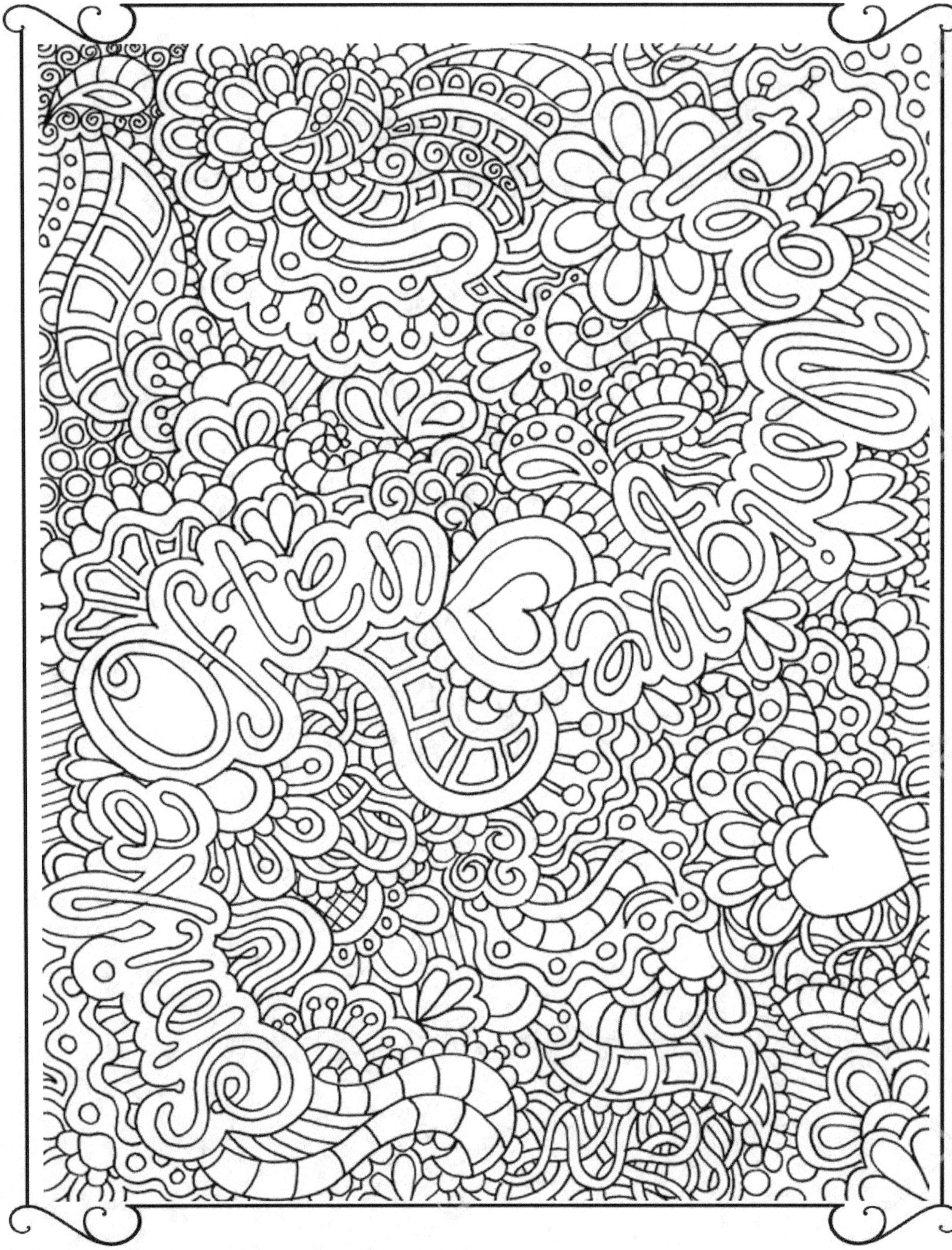
Often

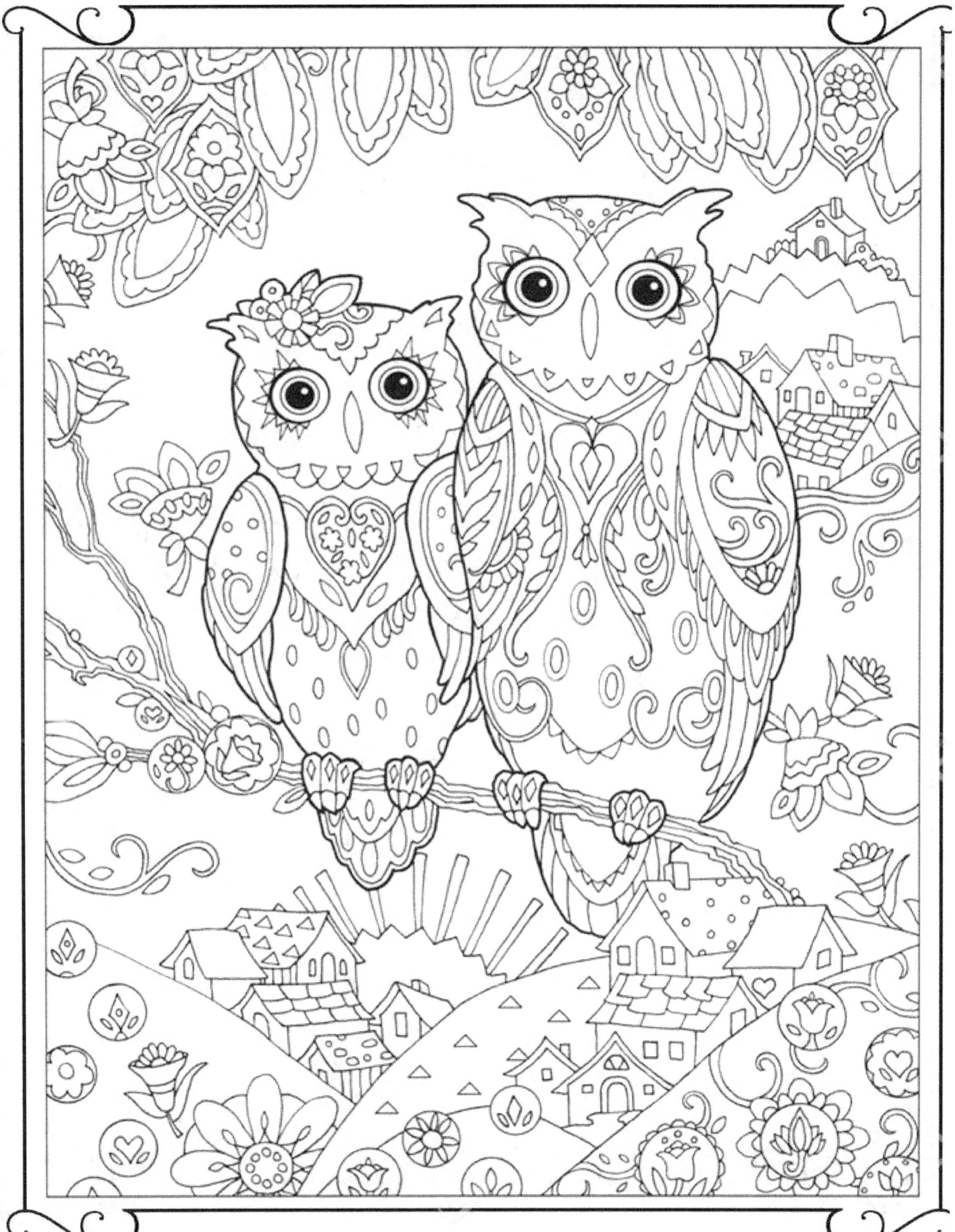

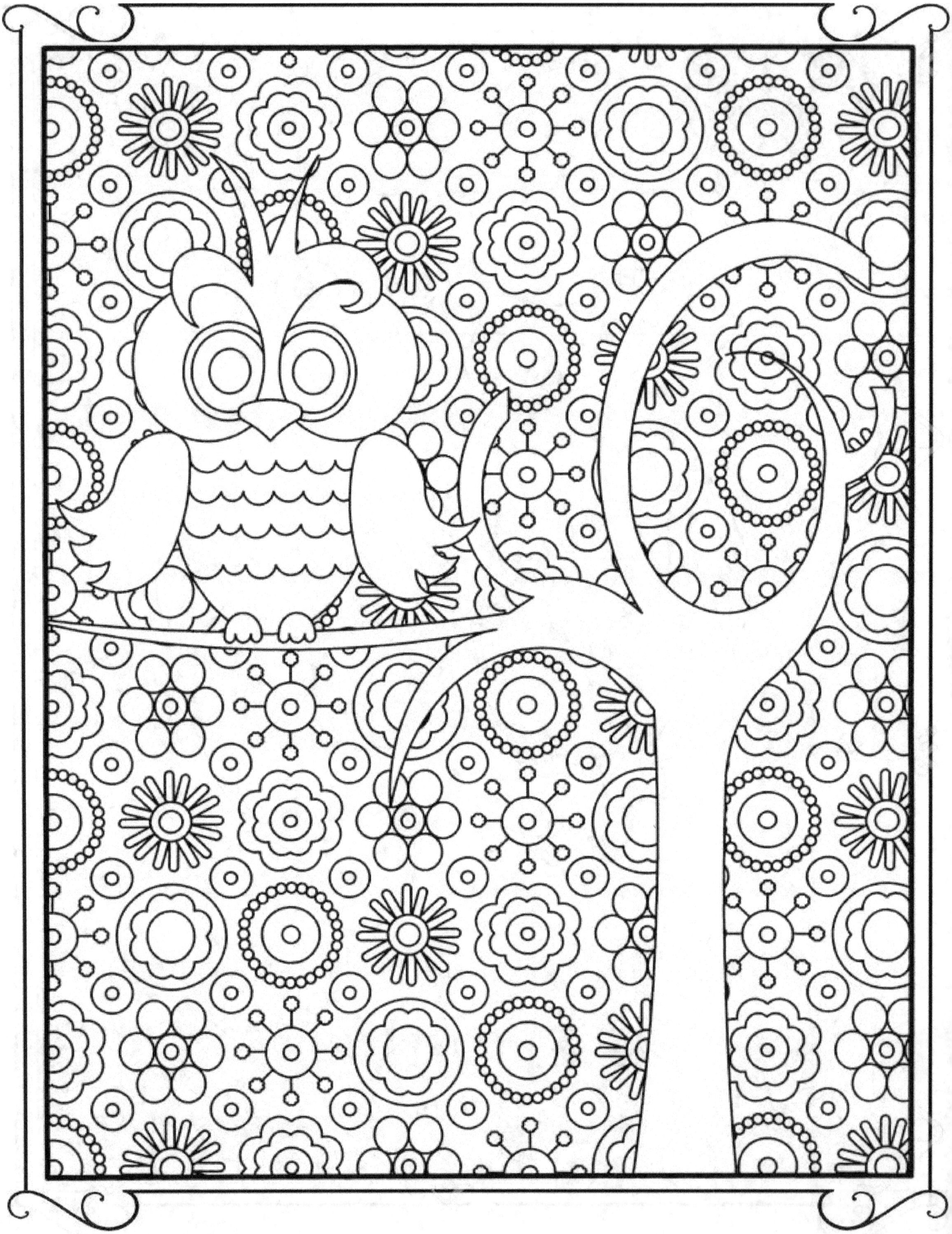

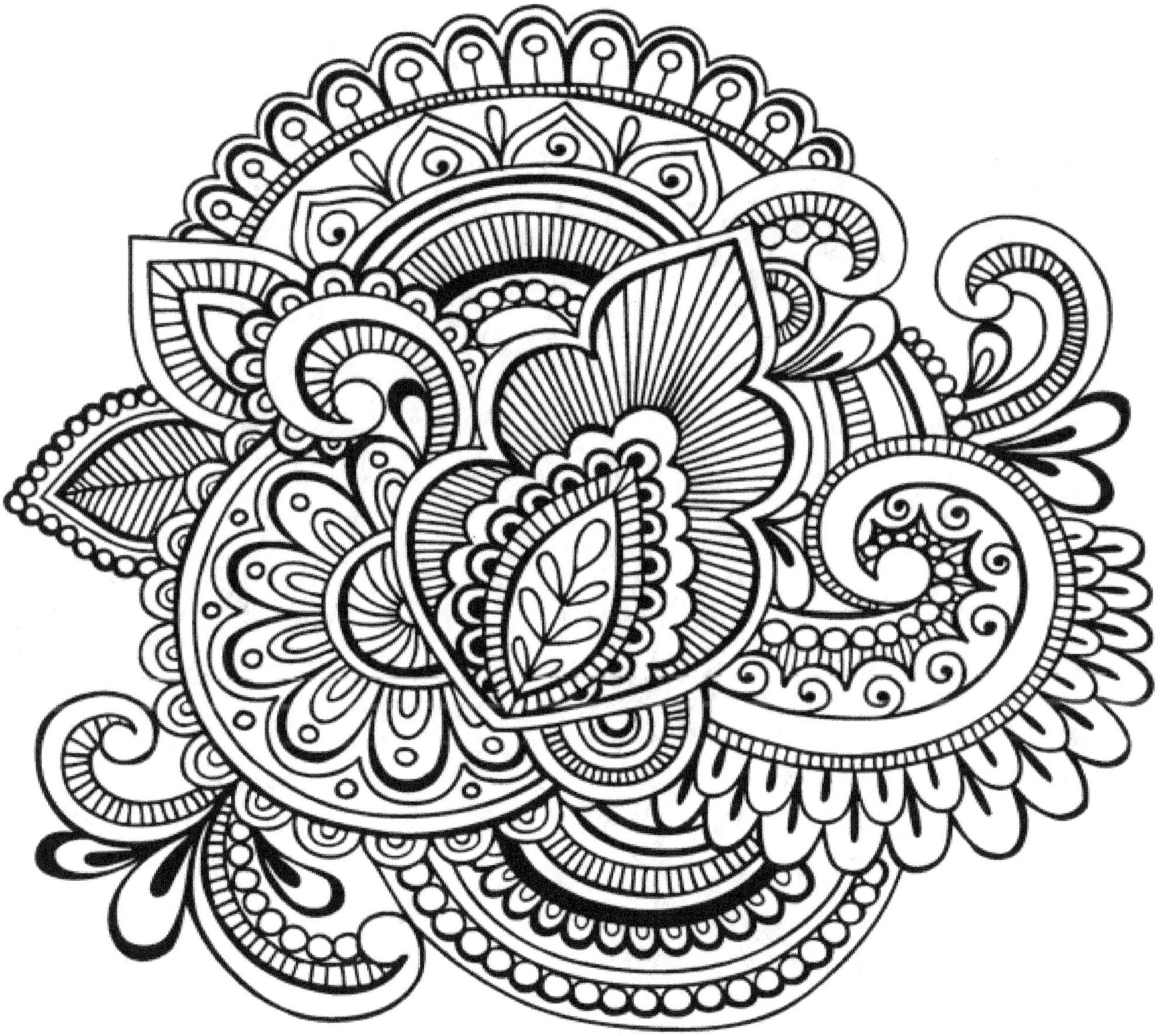

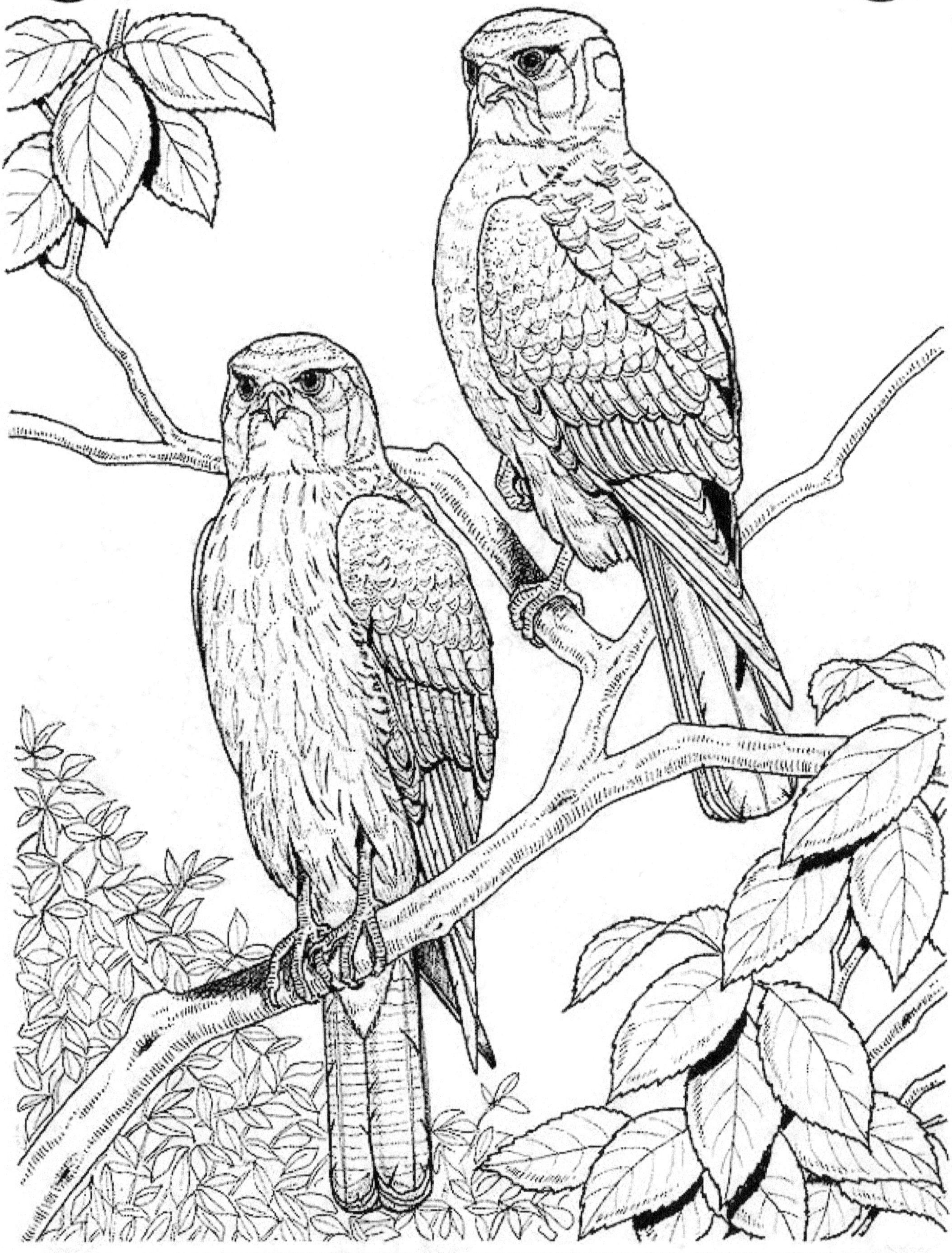

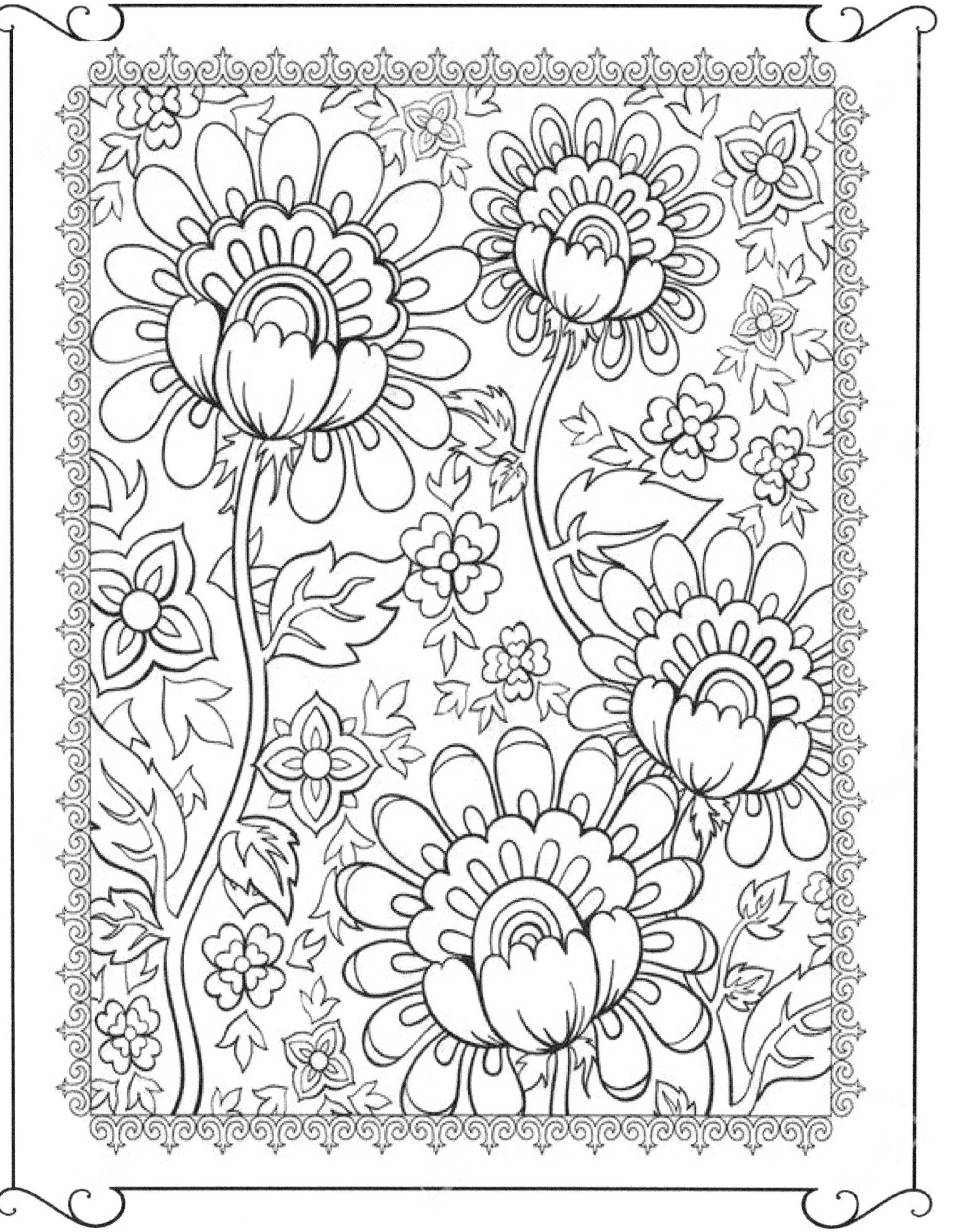

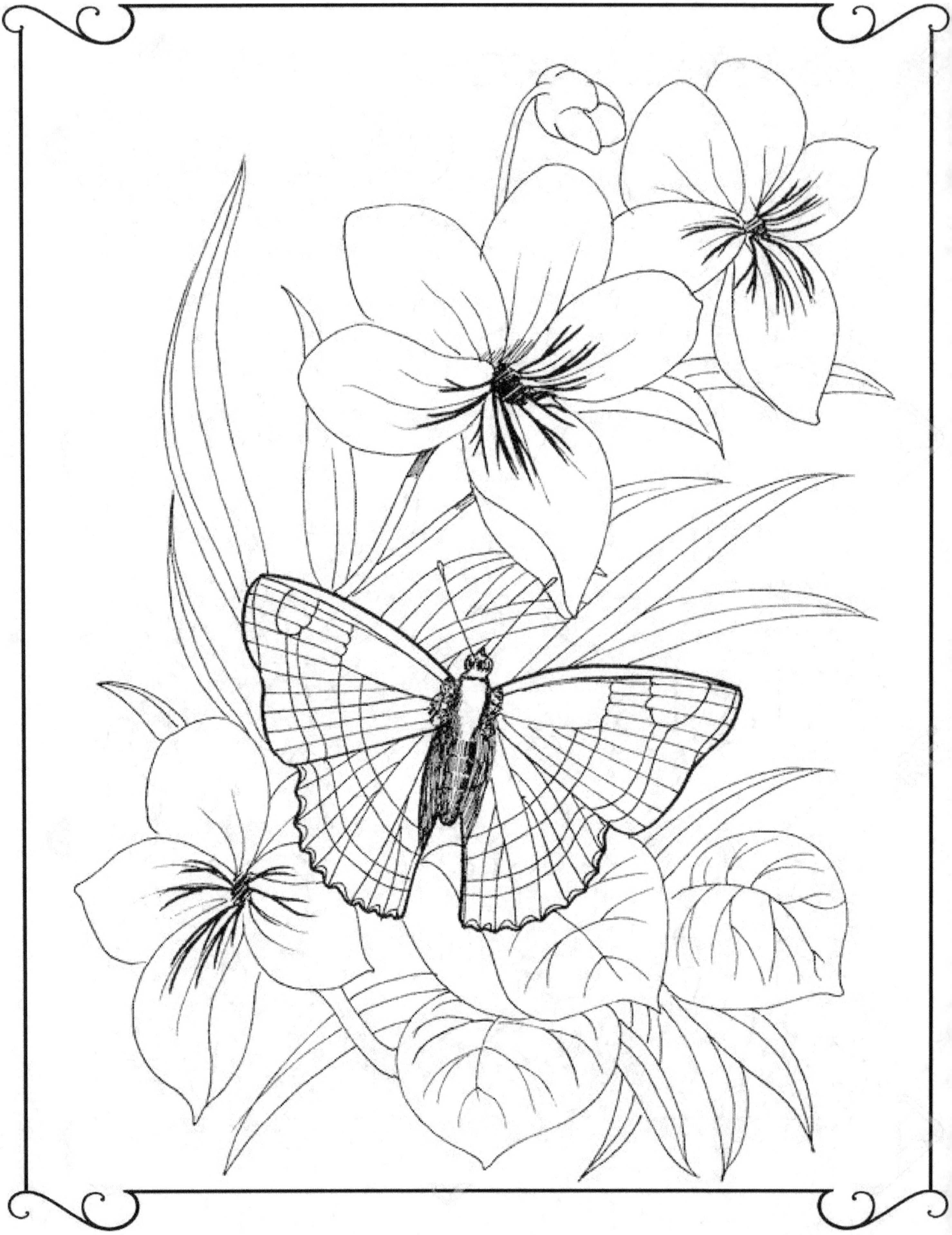

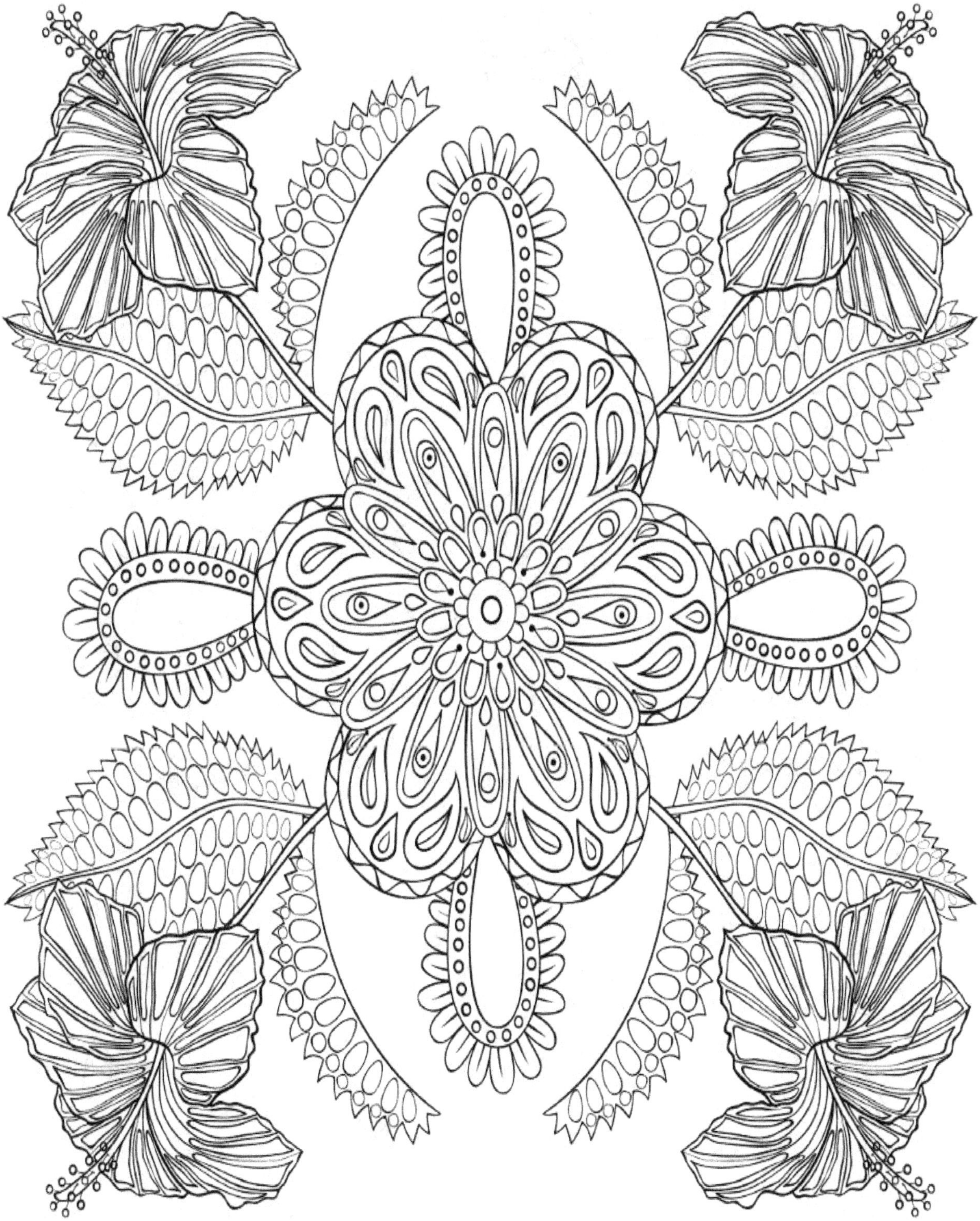

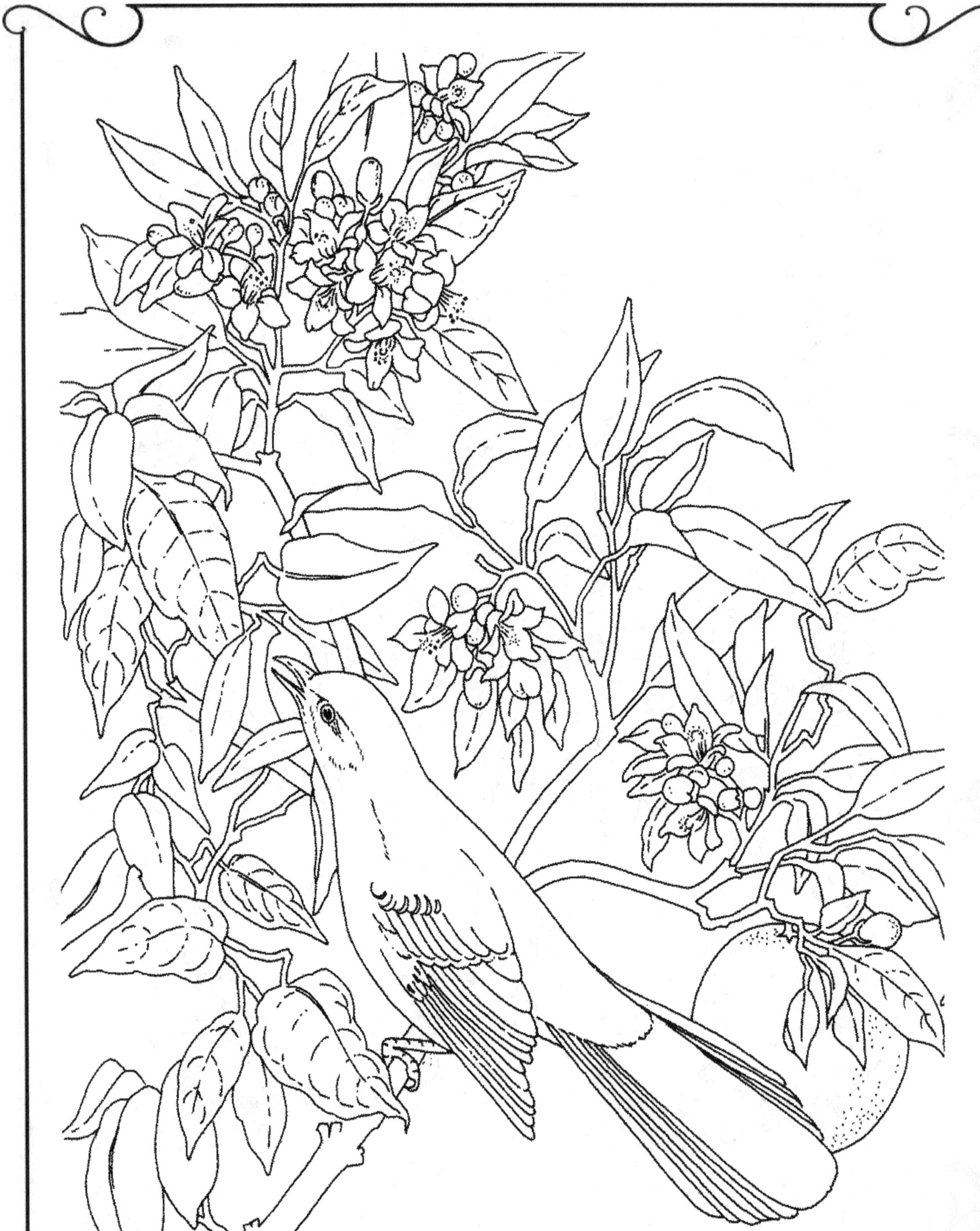

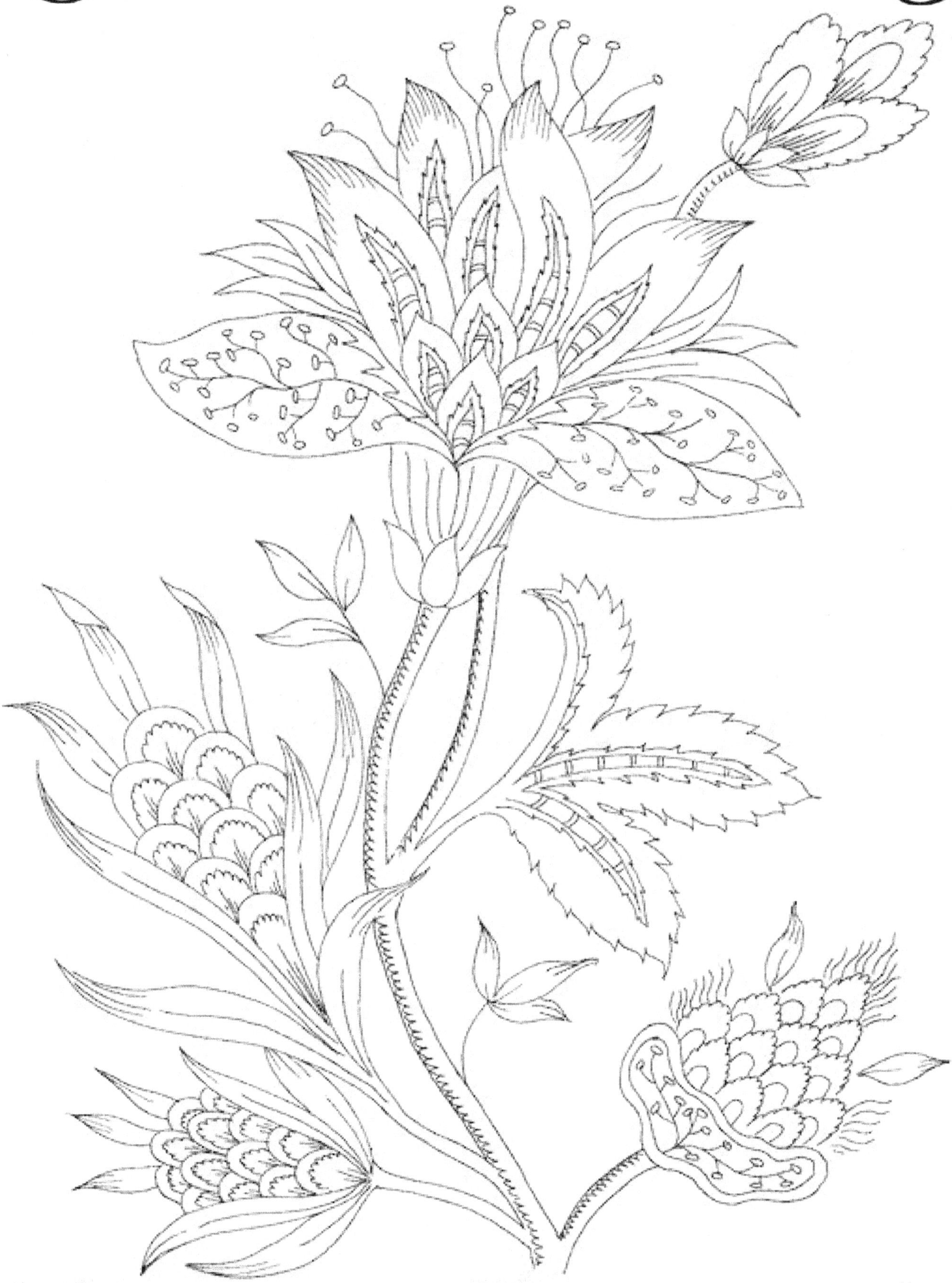

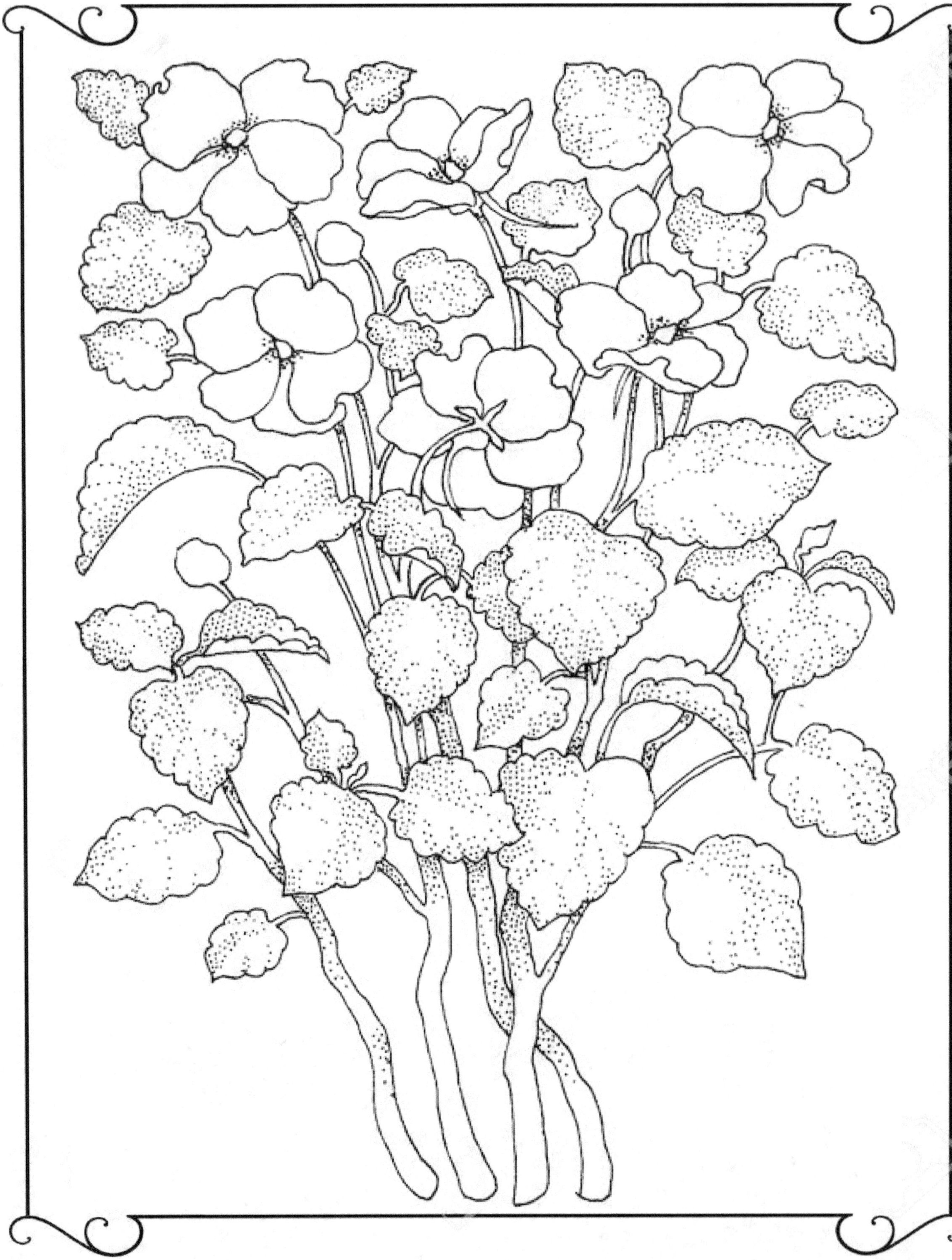

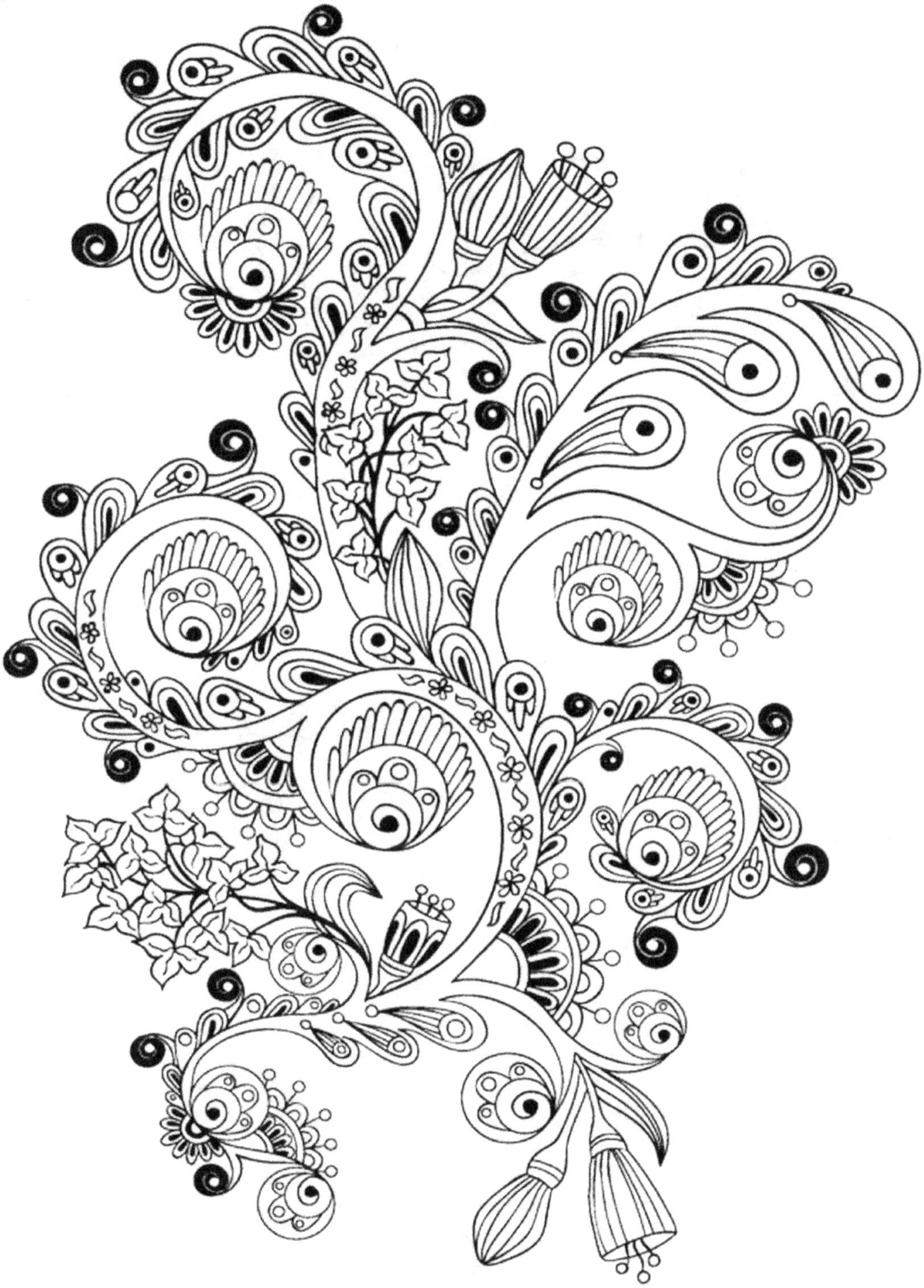

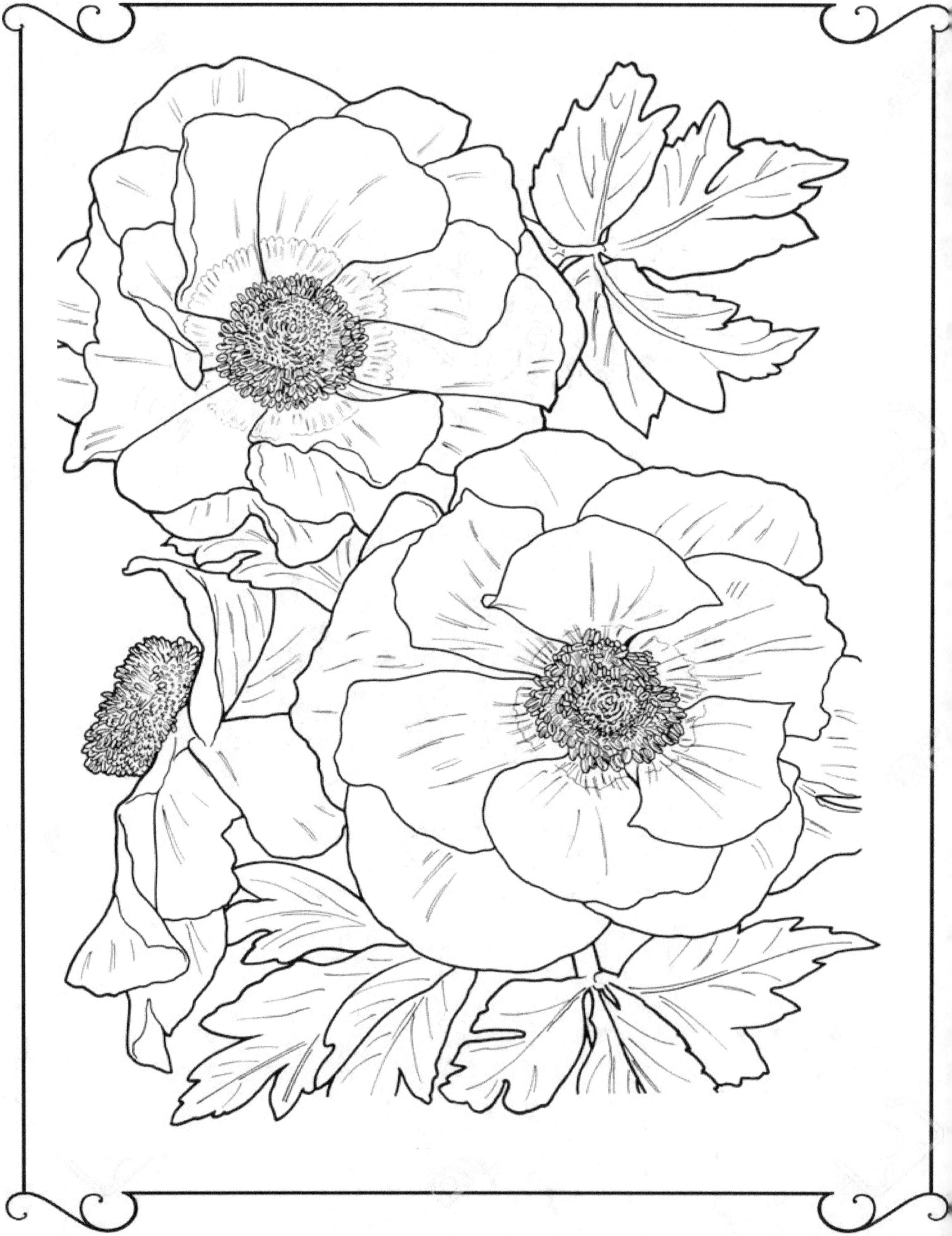

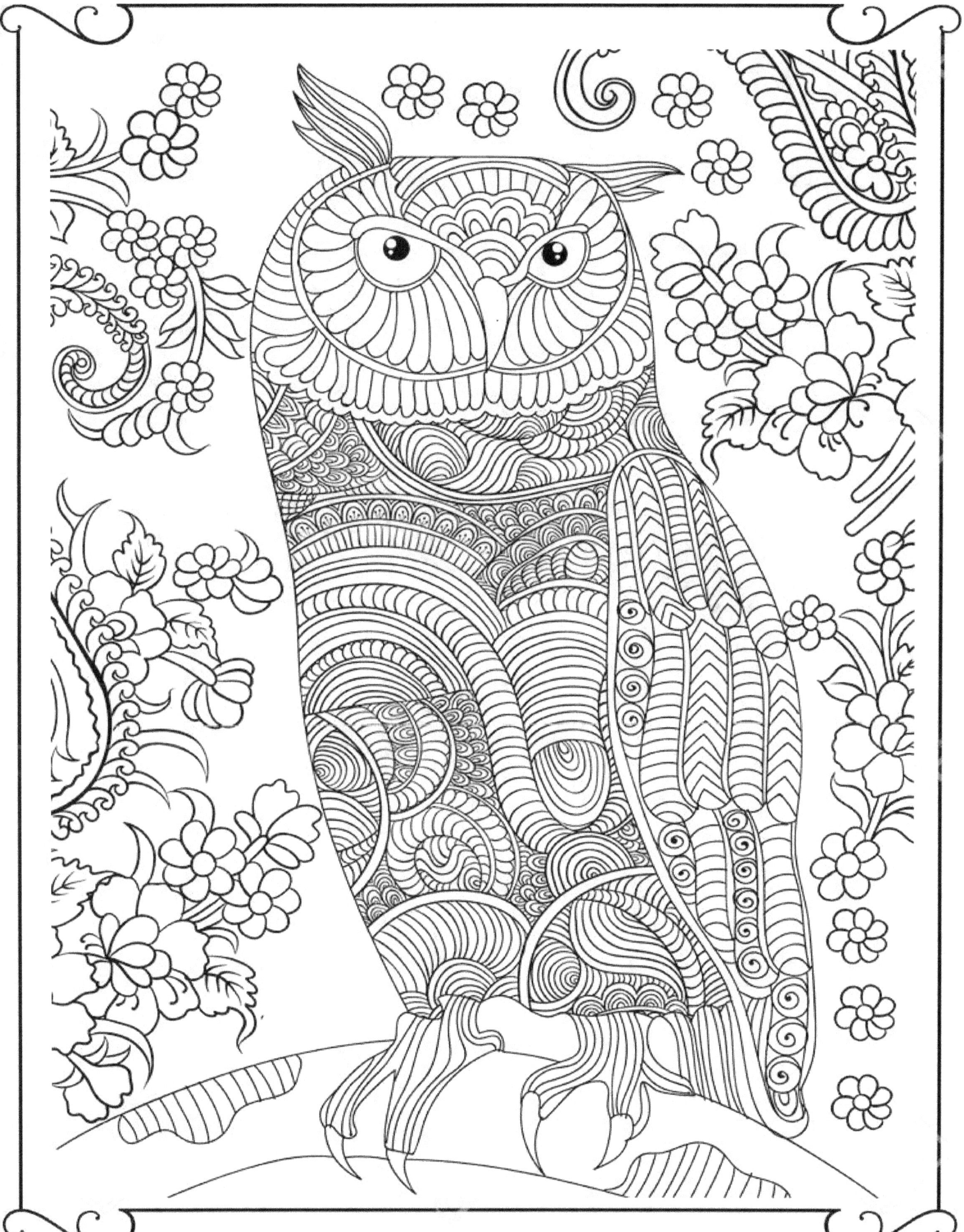

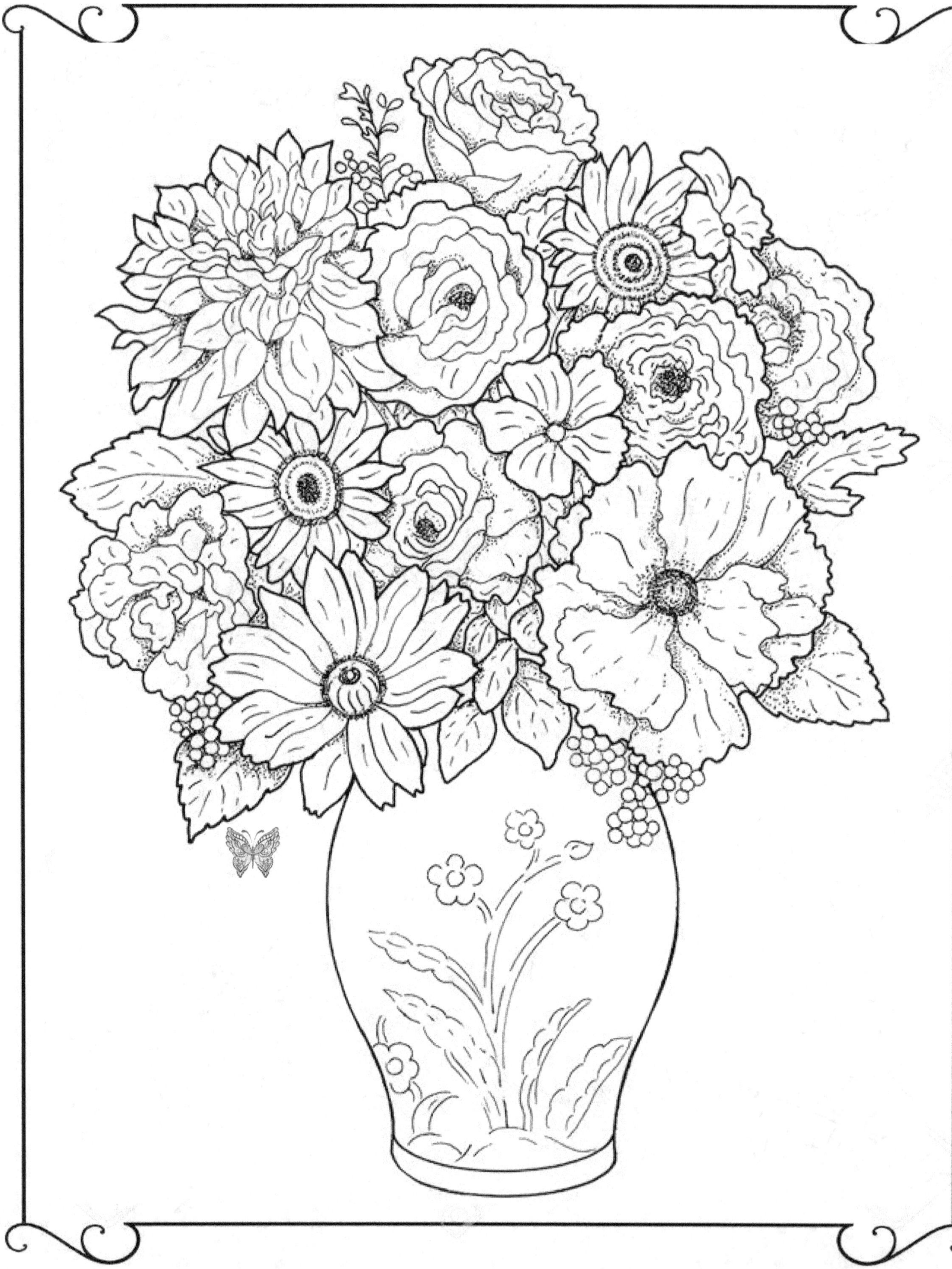

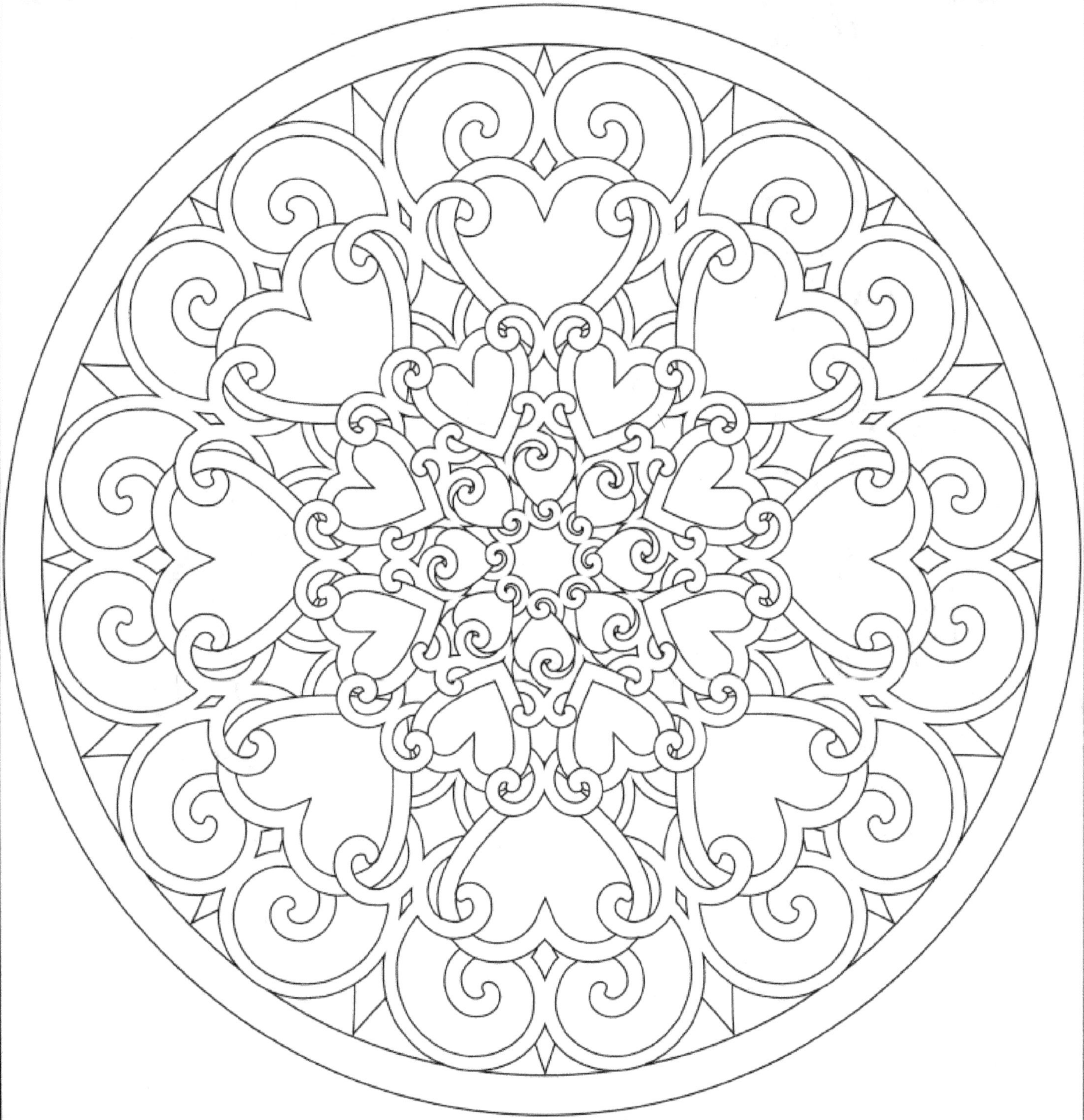

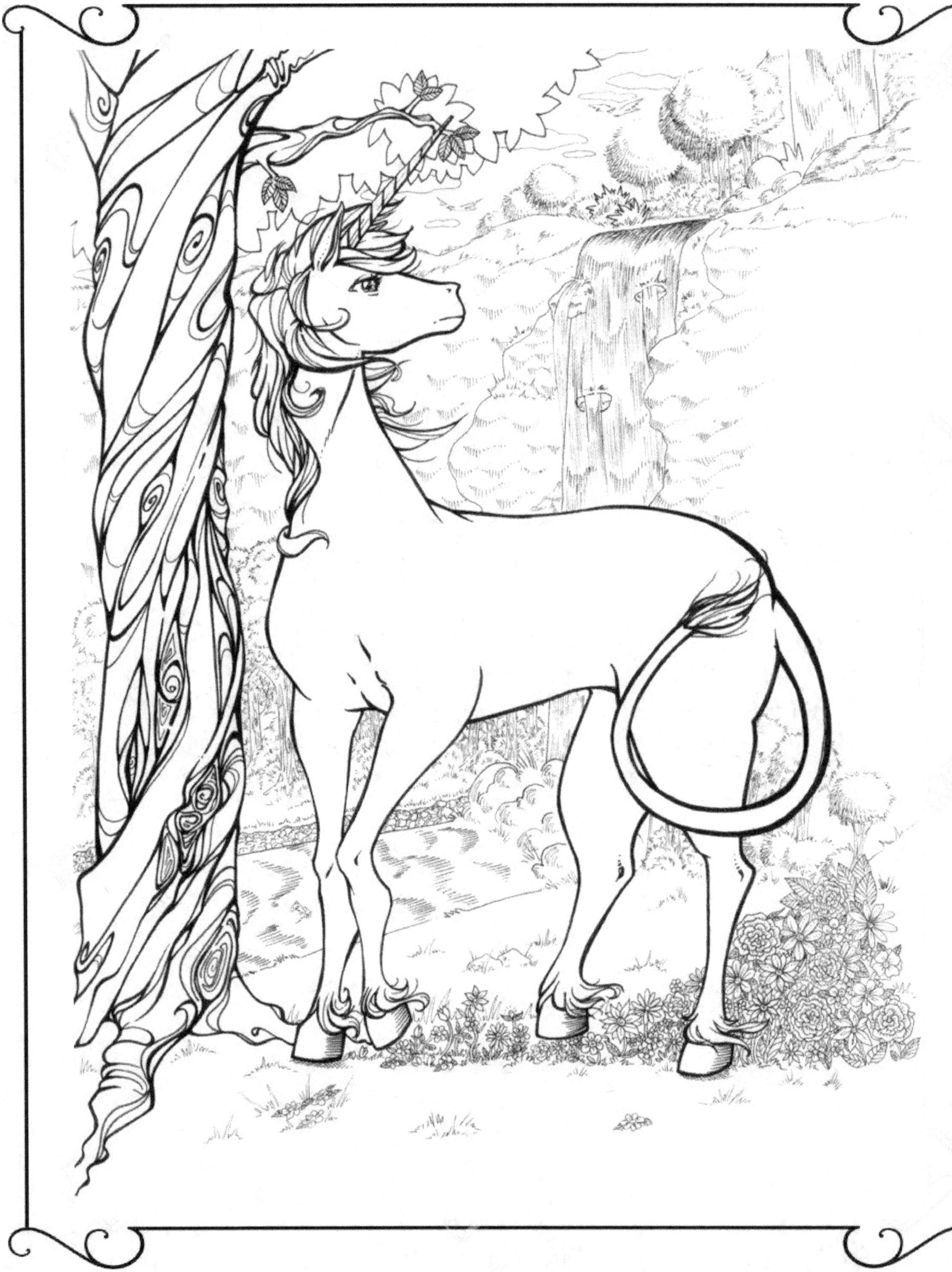

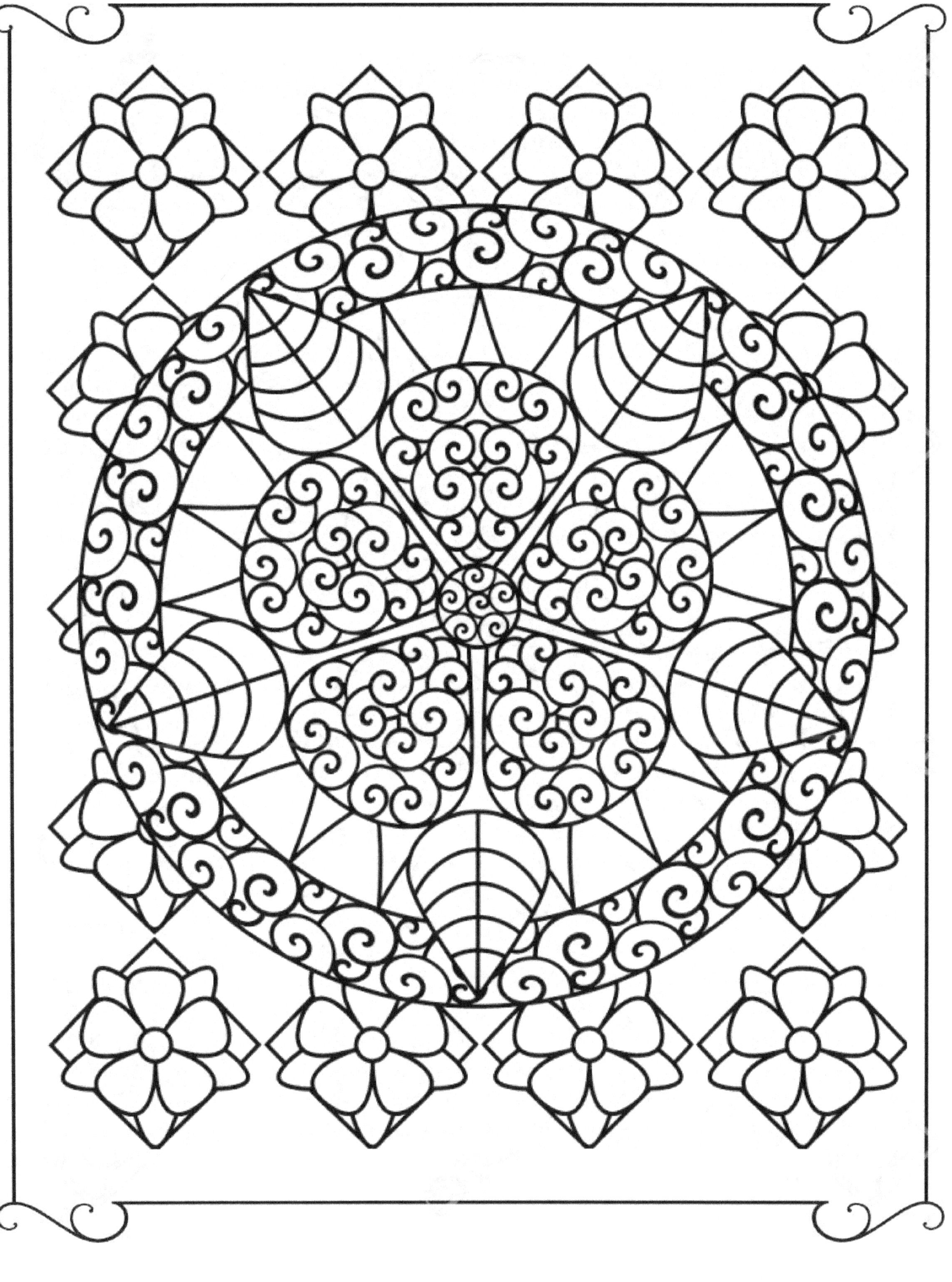

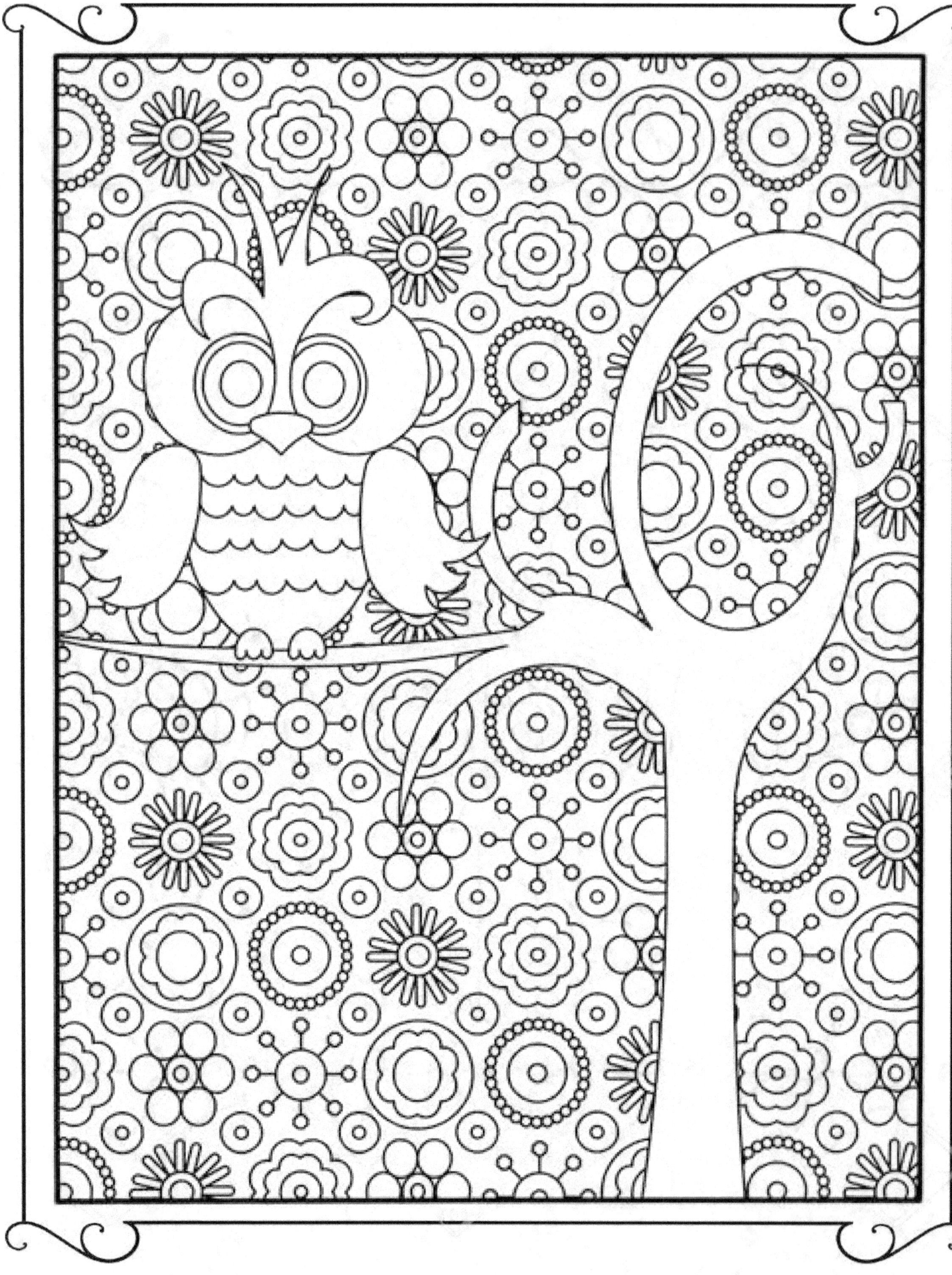

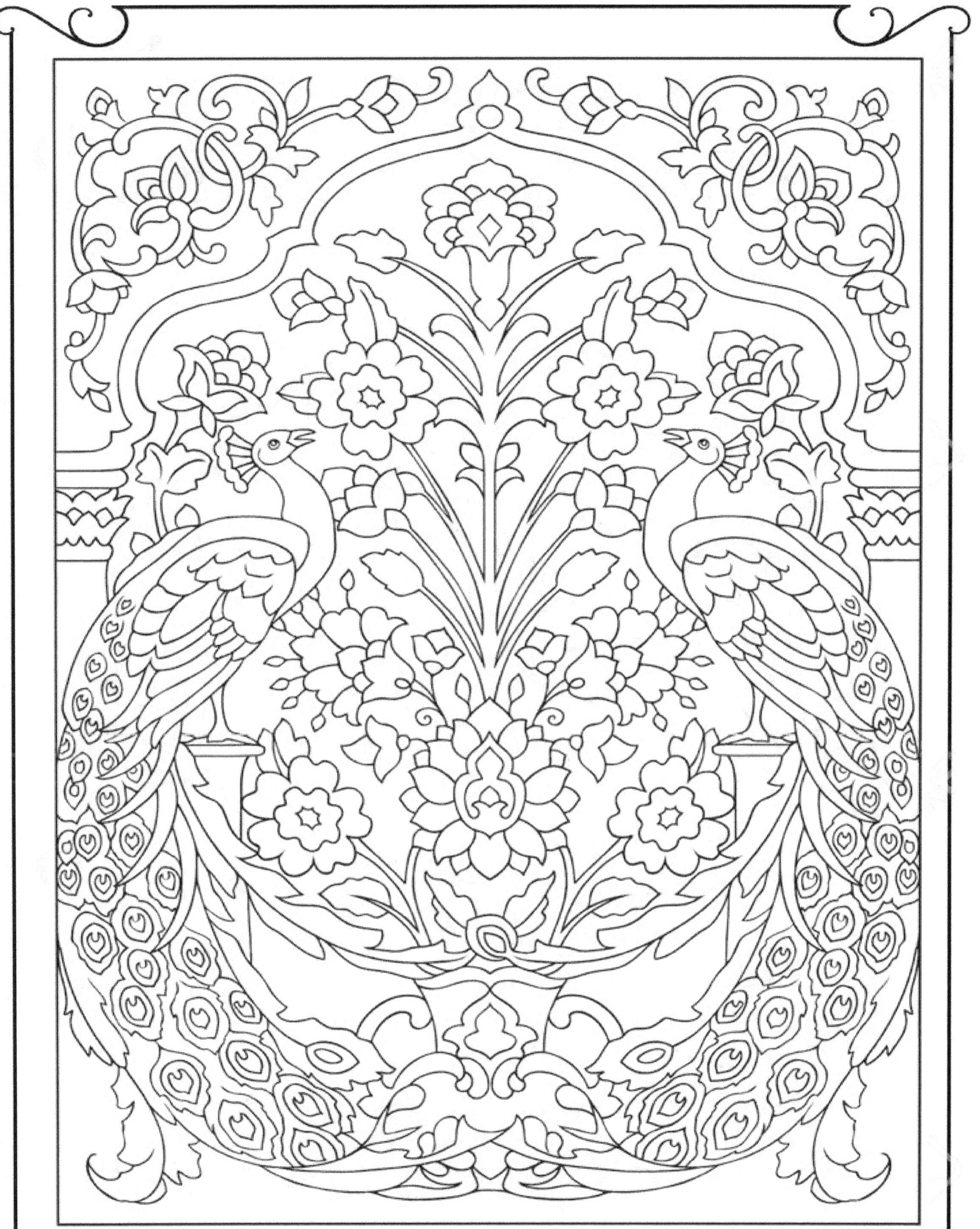

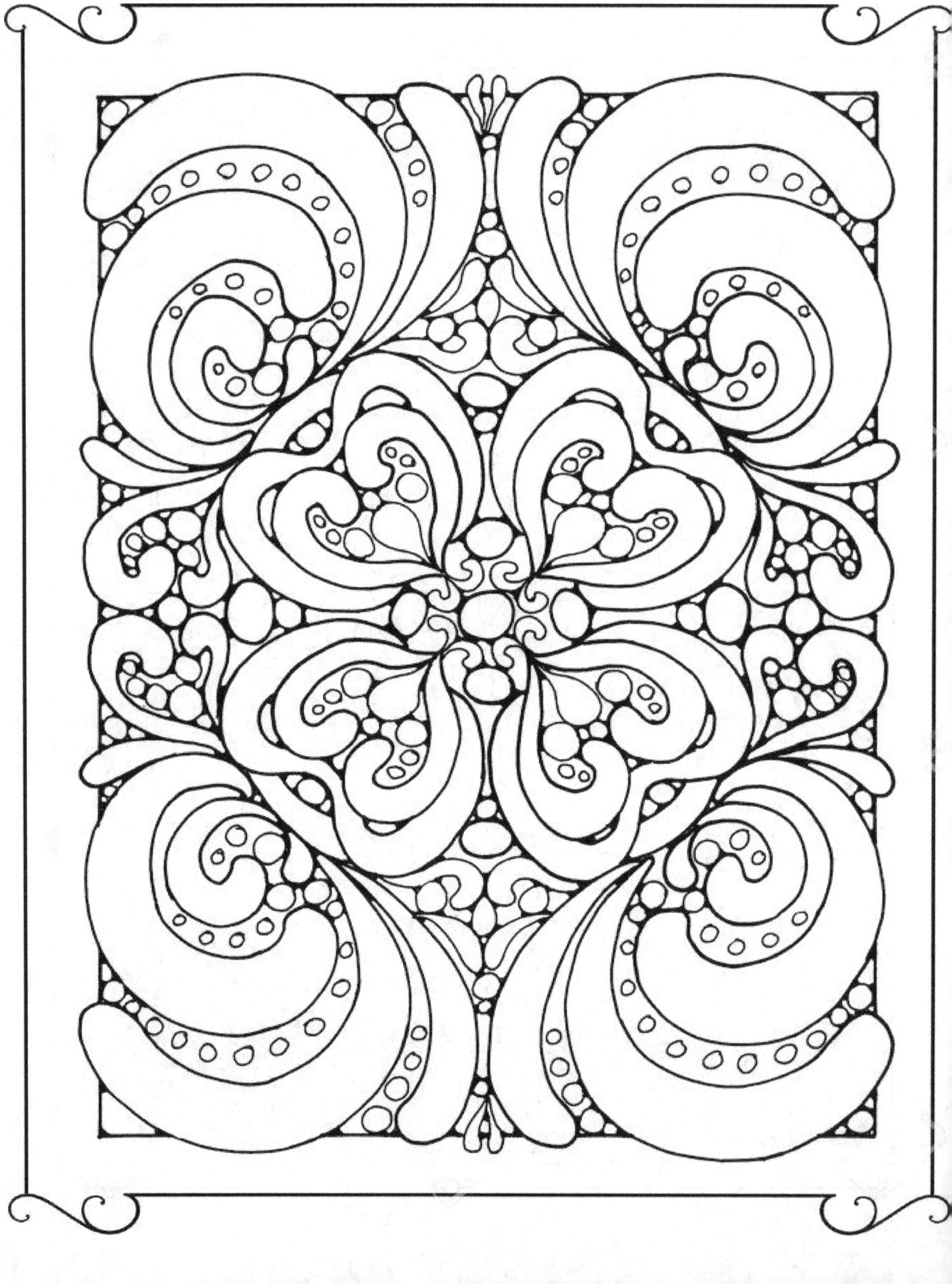

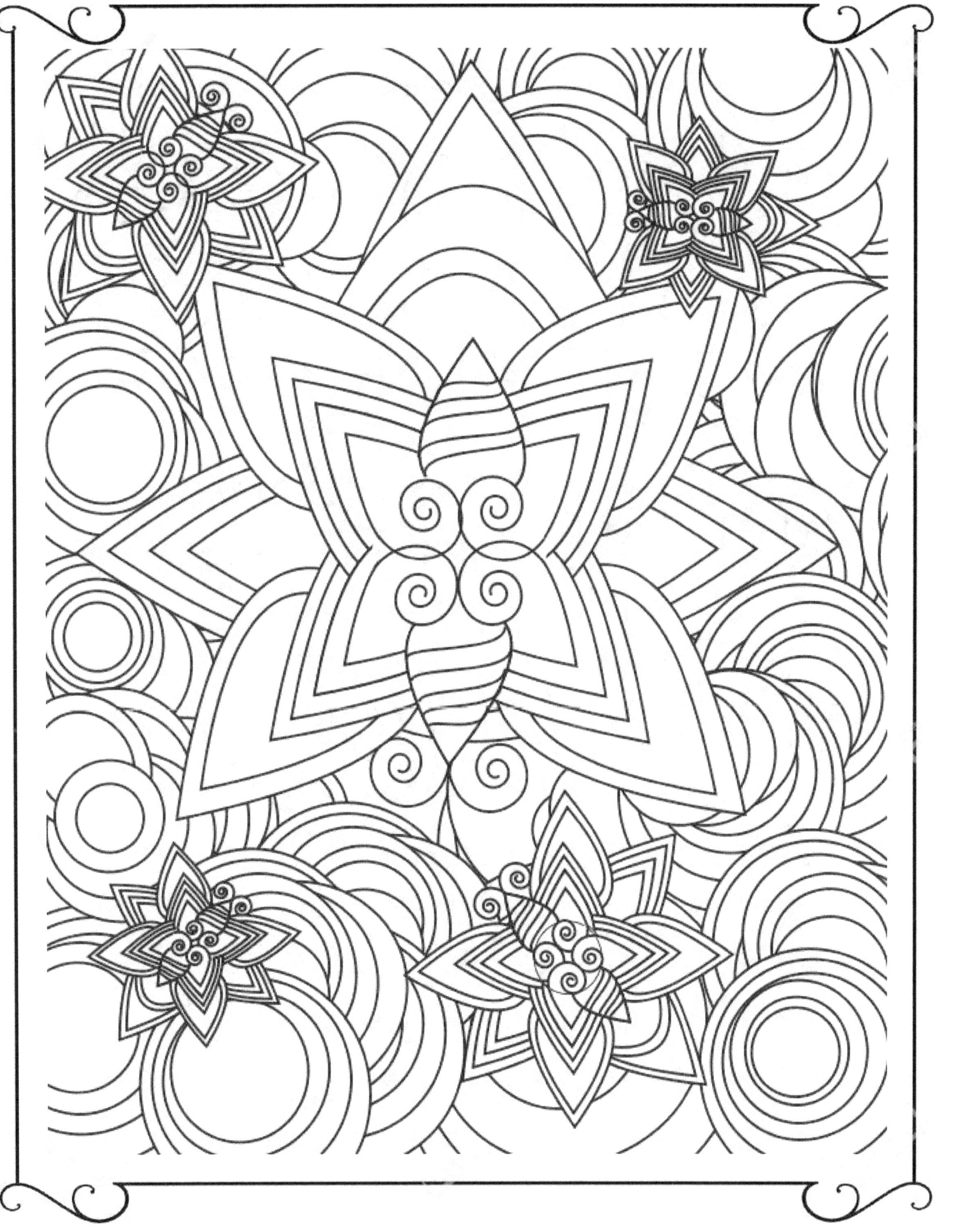

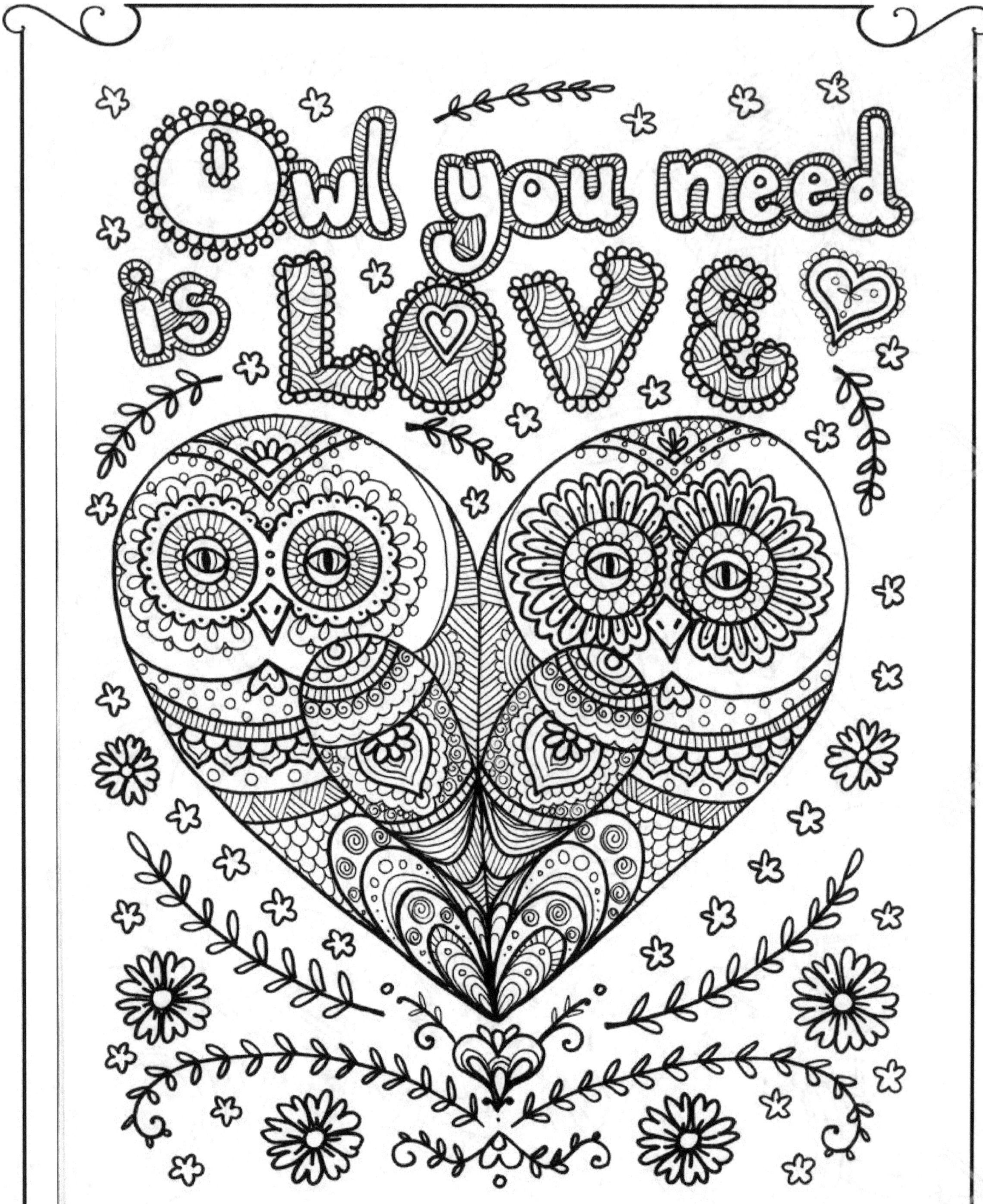
Owl you need is LOVE

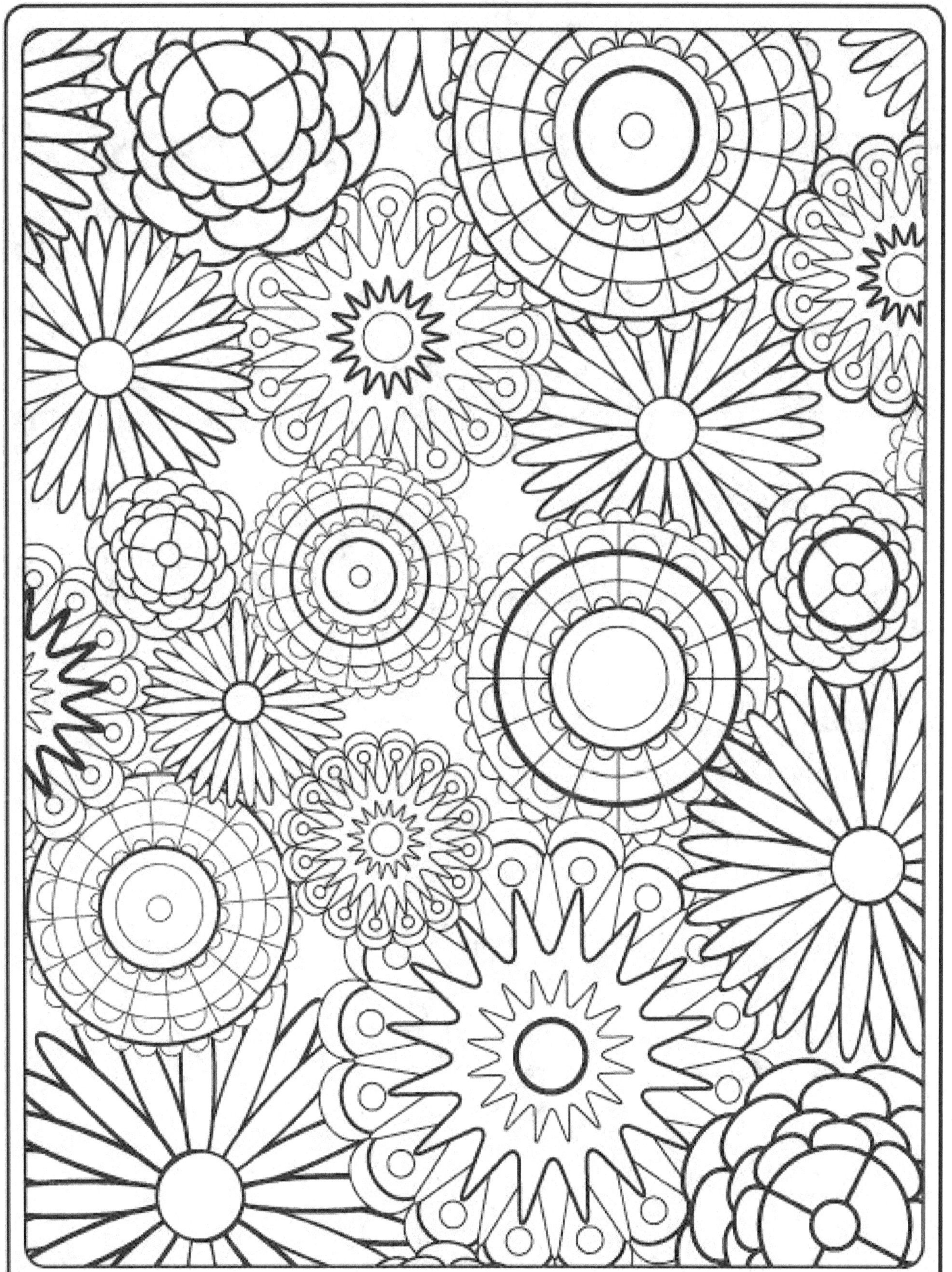

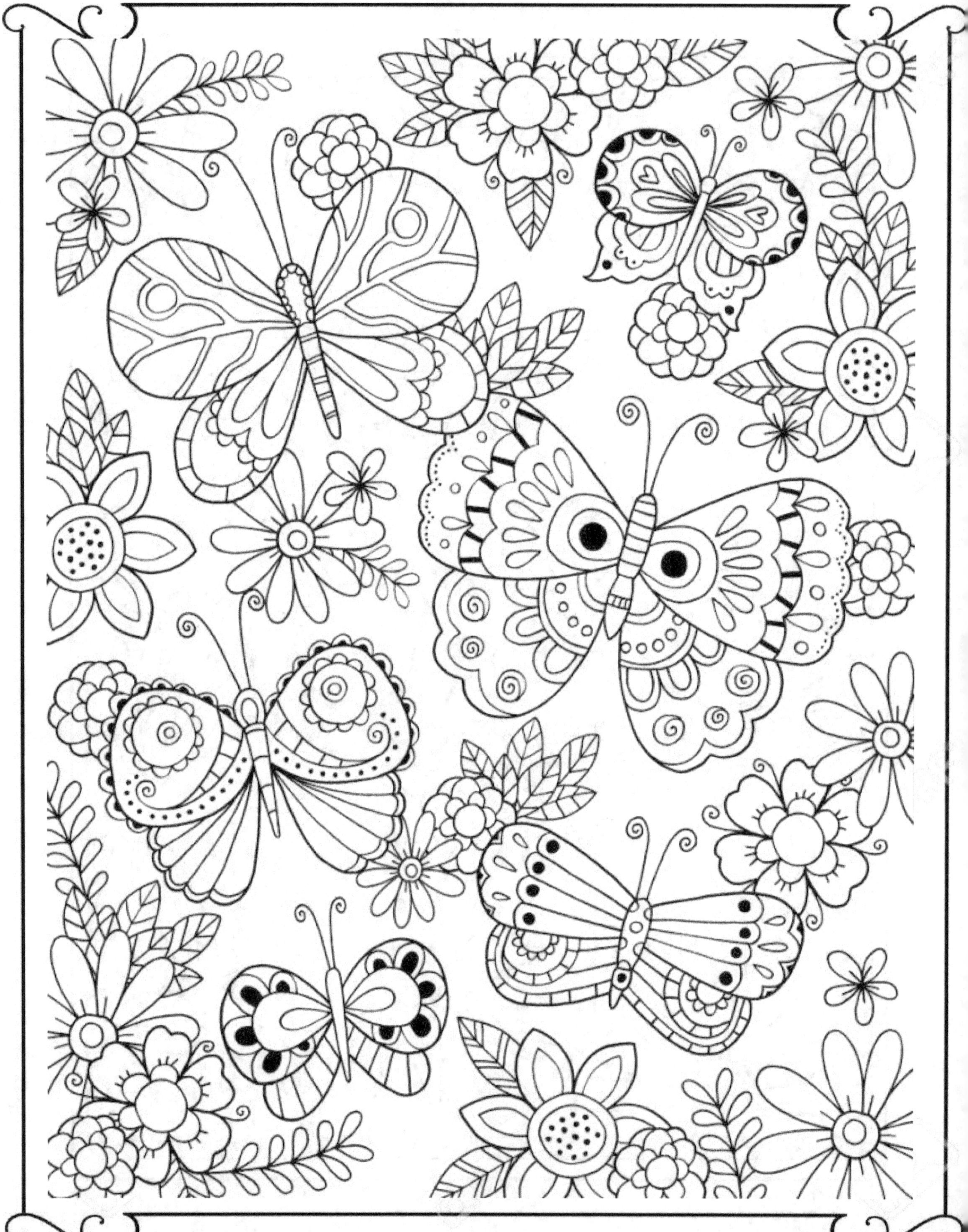

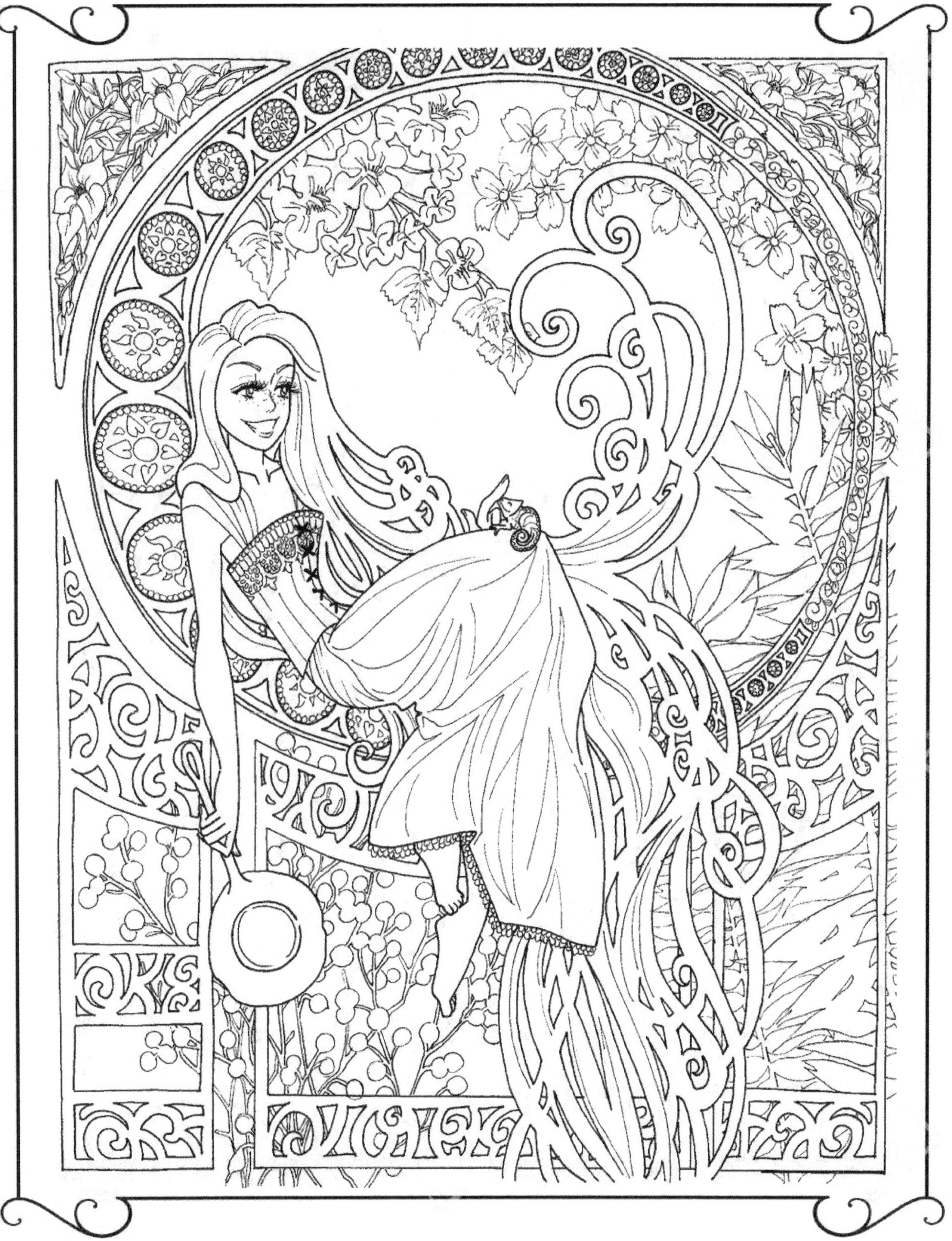

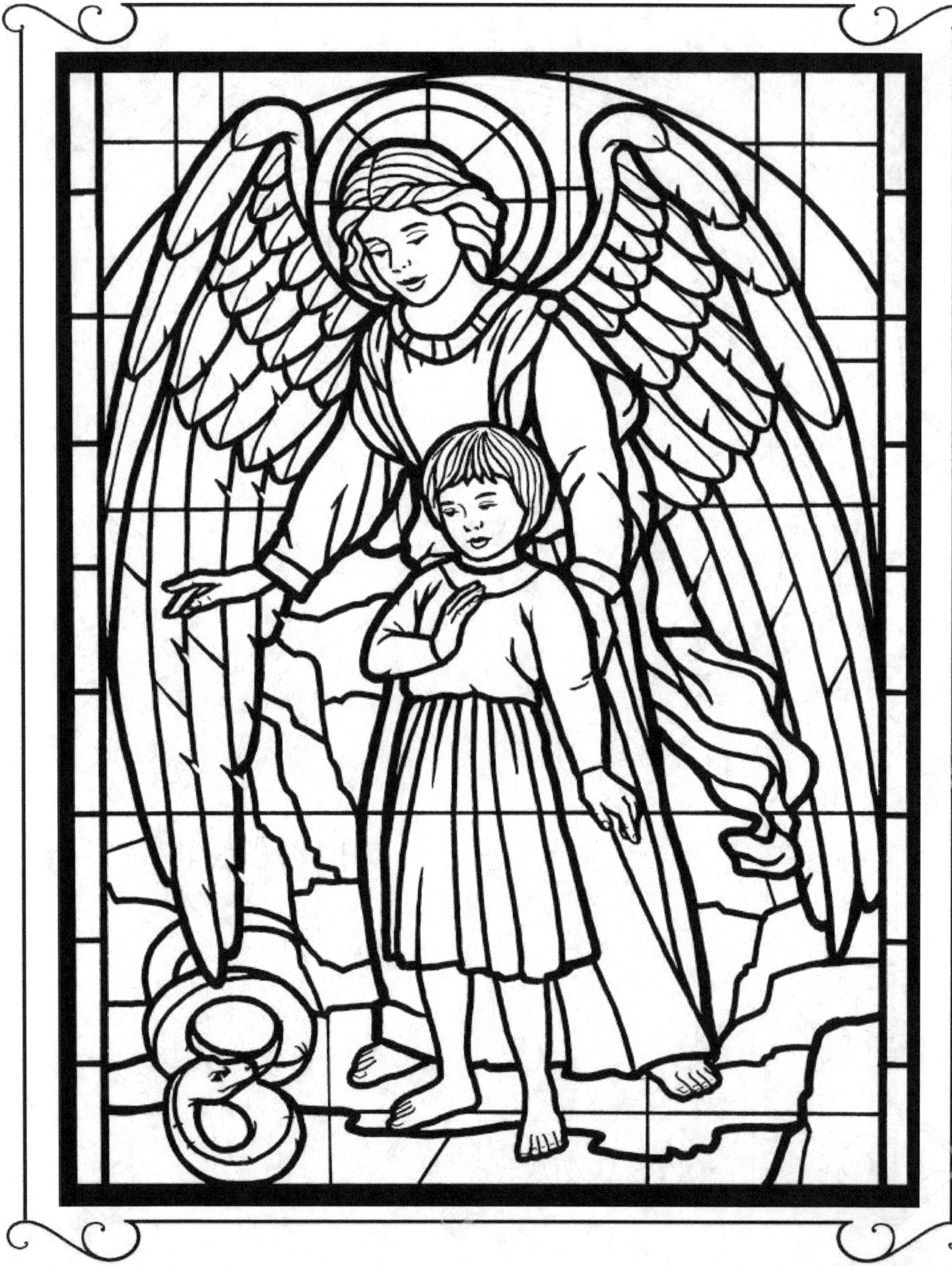

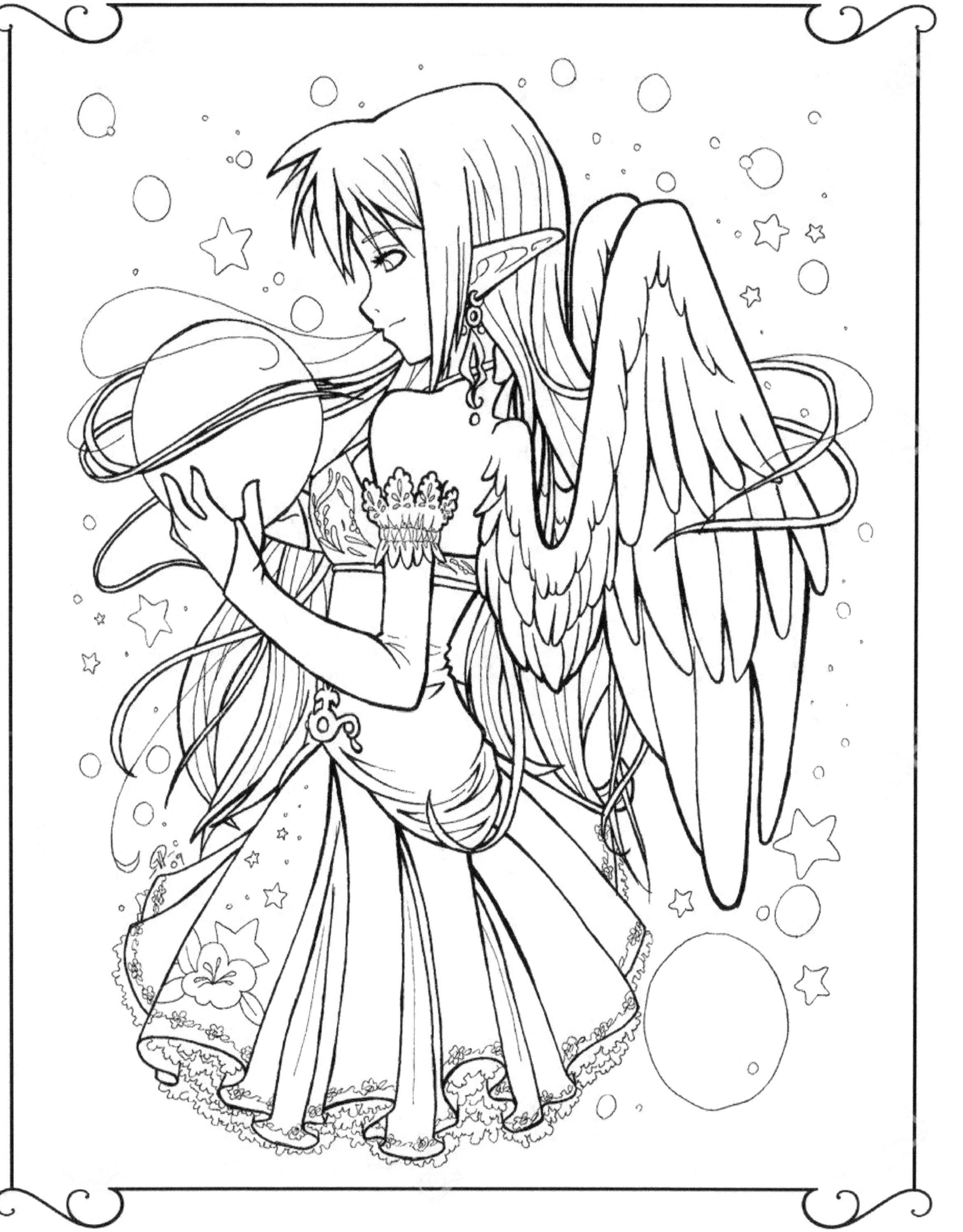

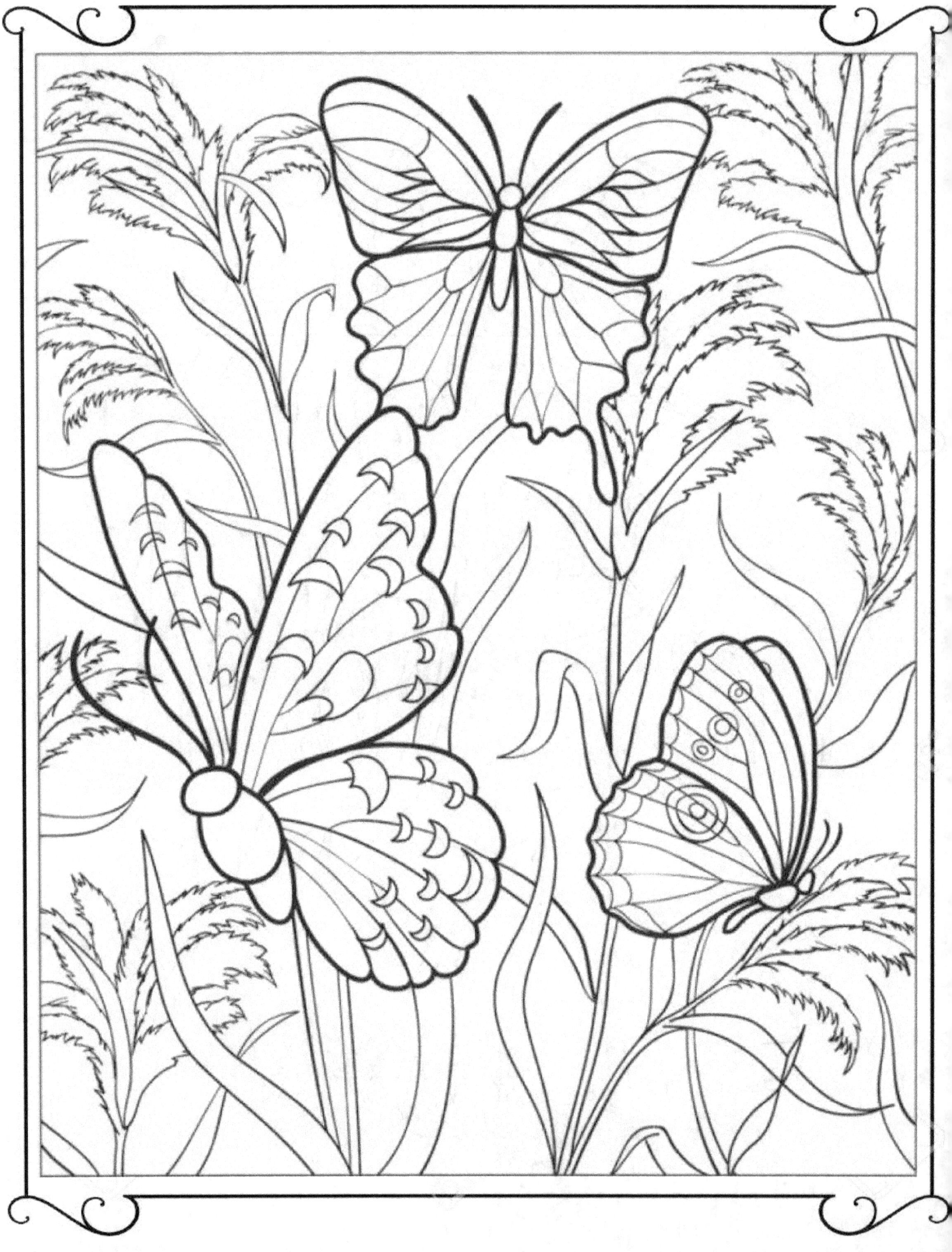

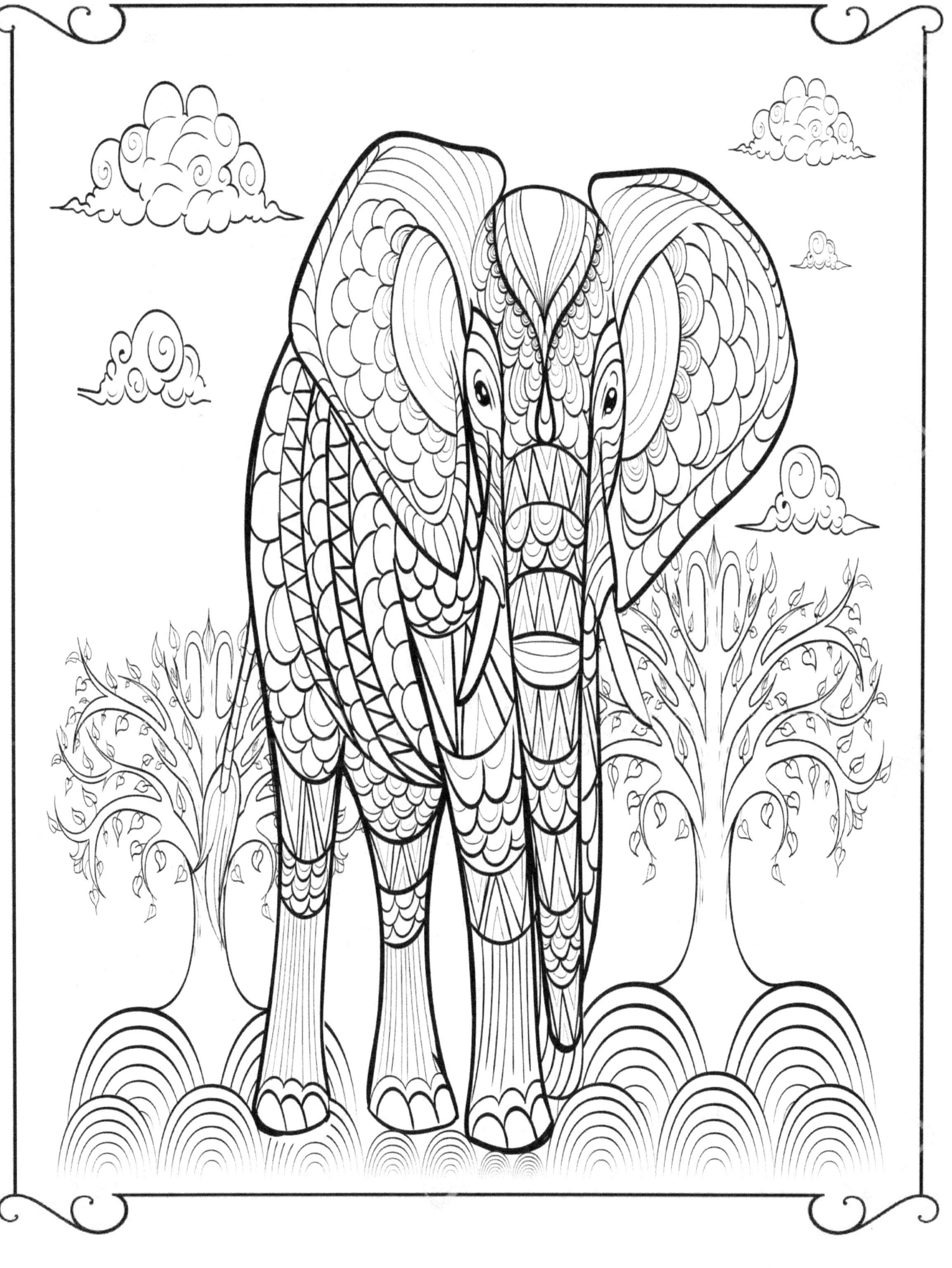

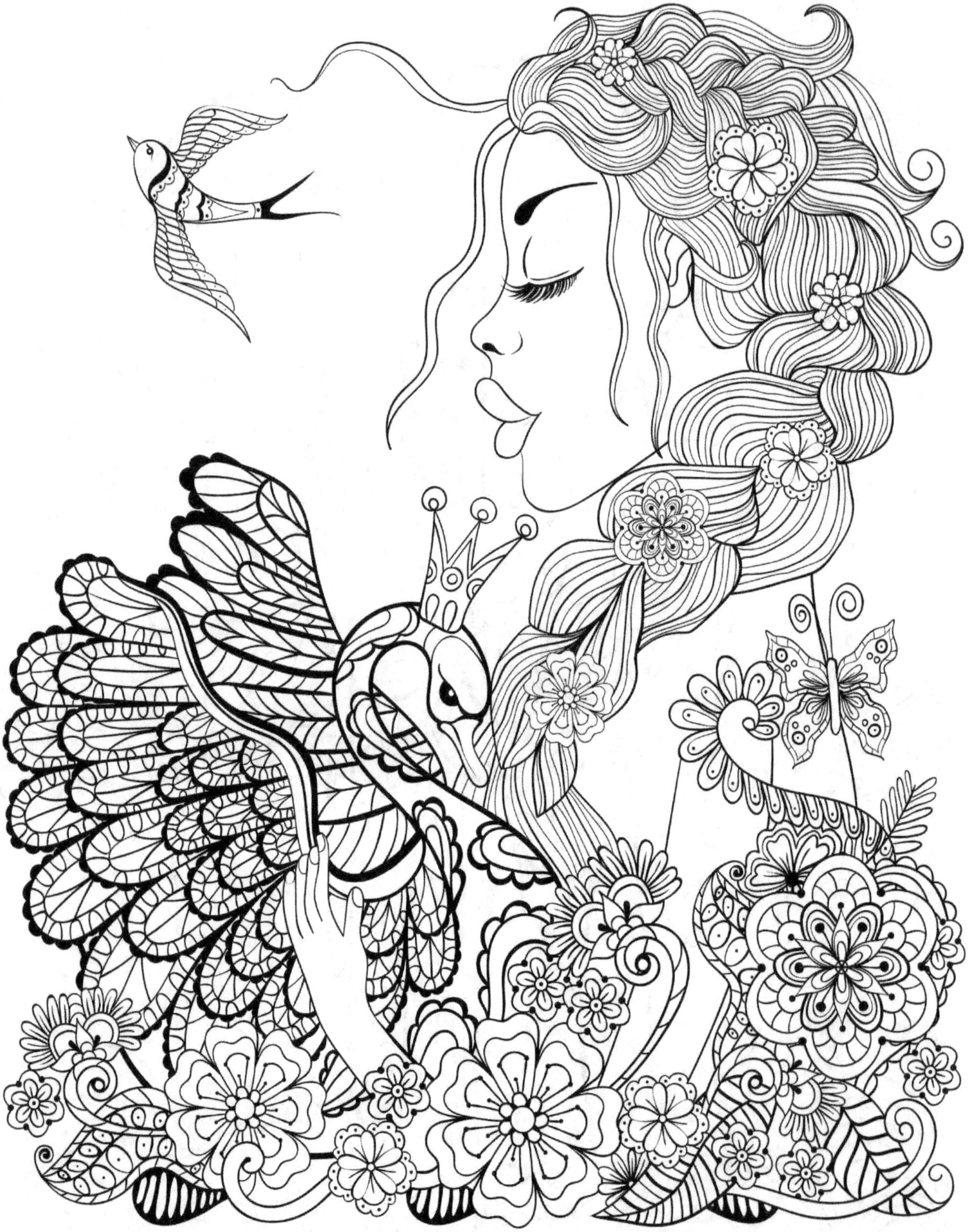

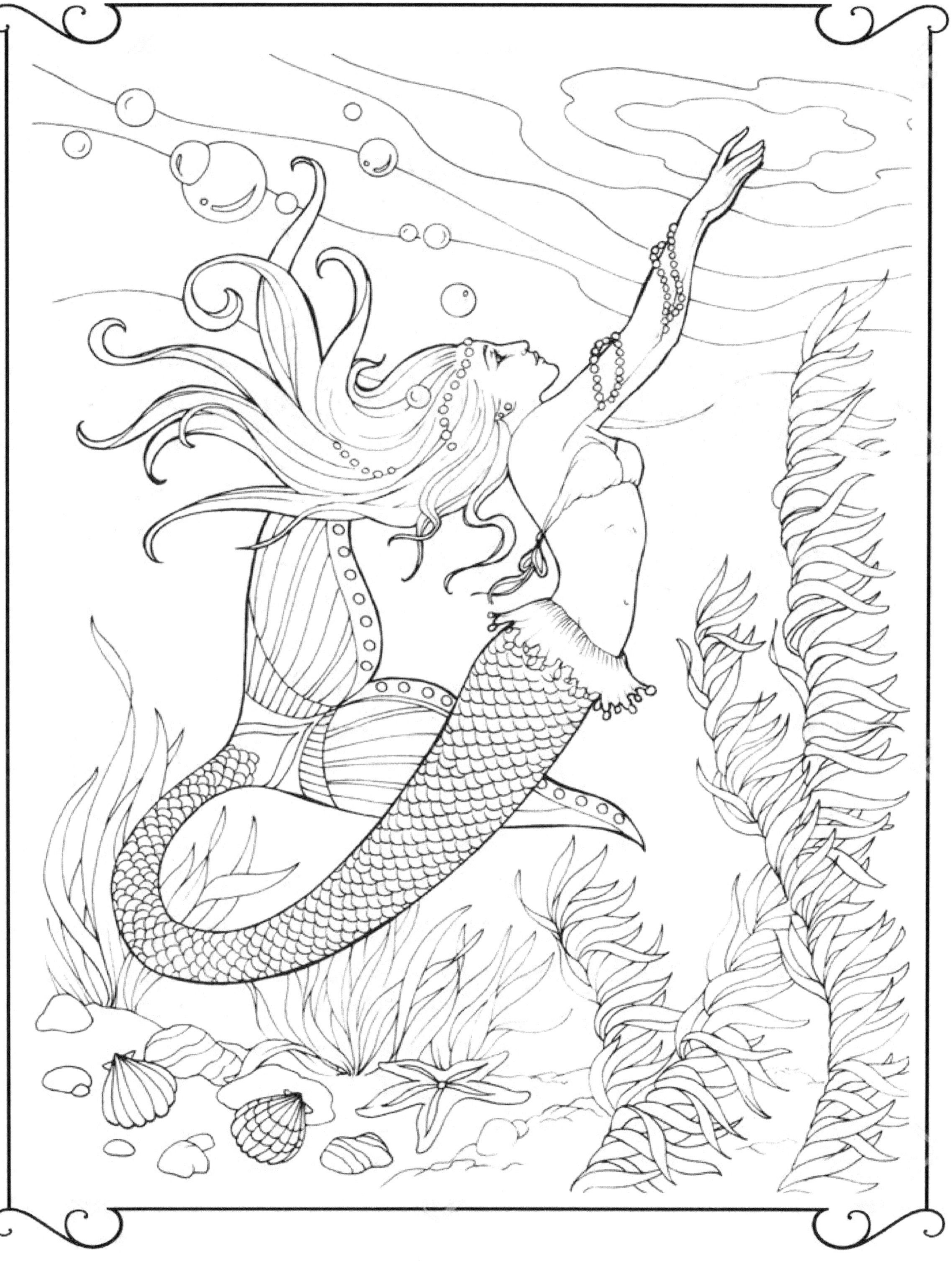

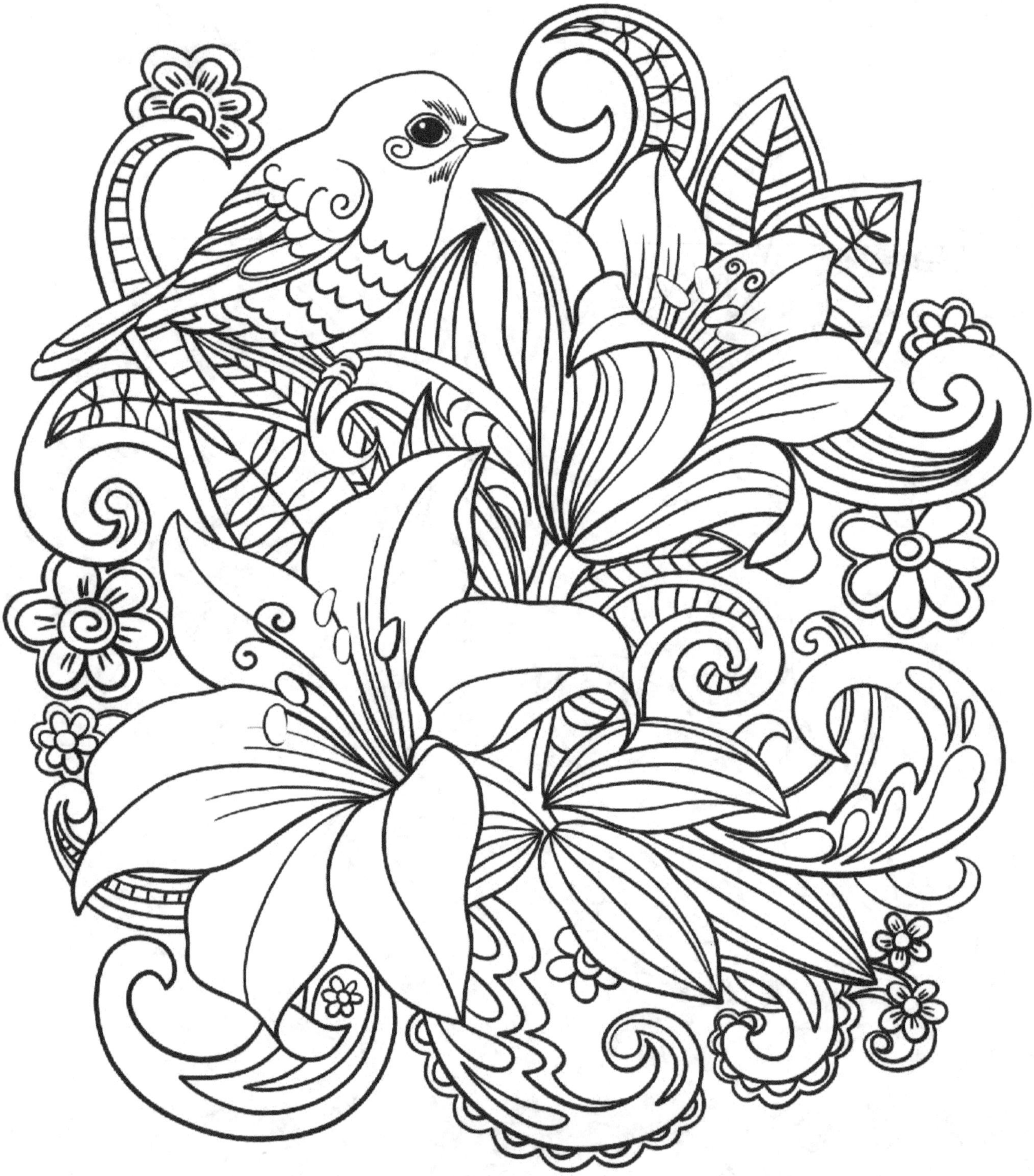

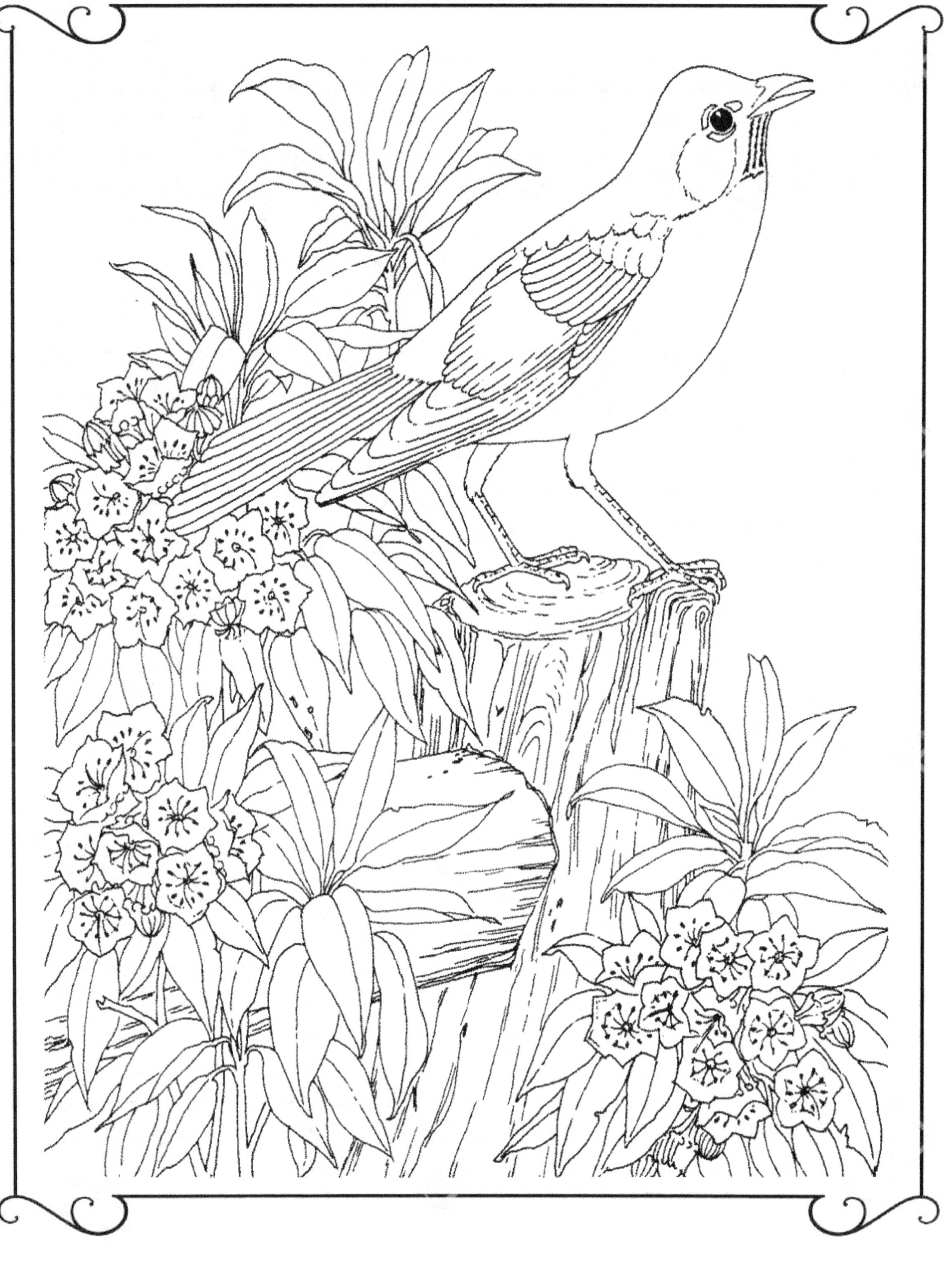

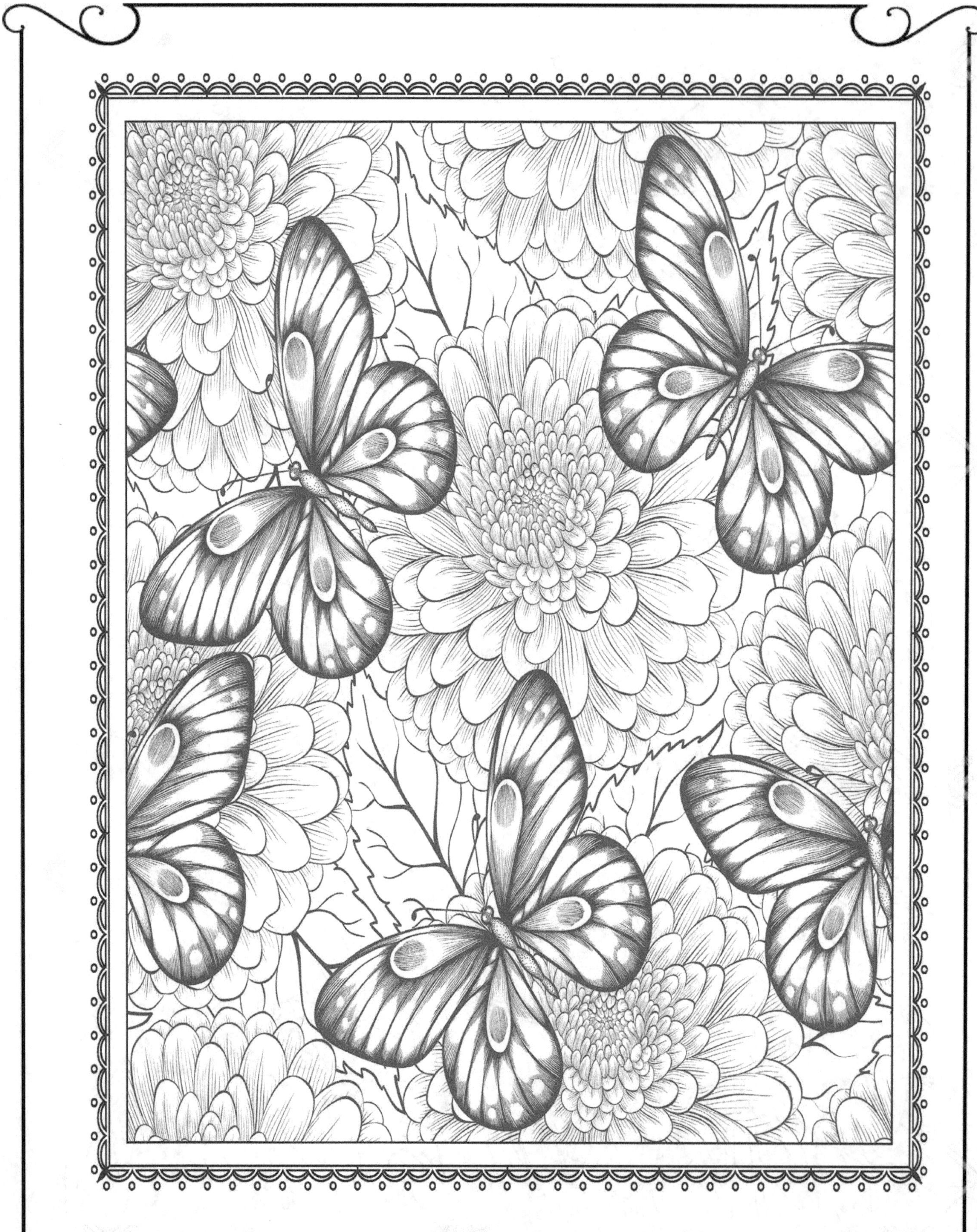

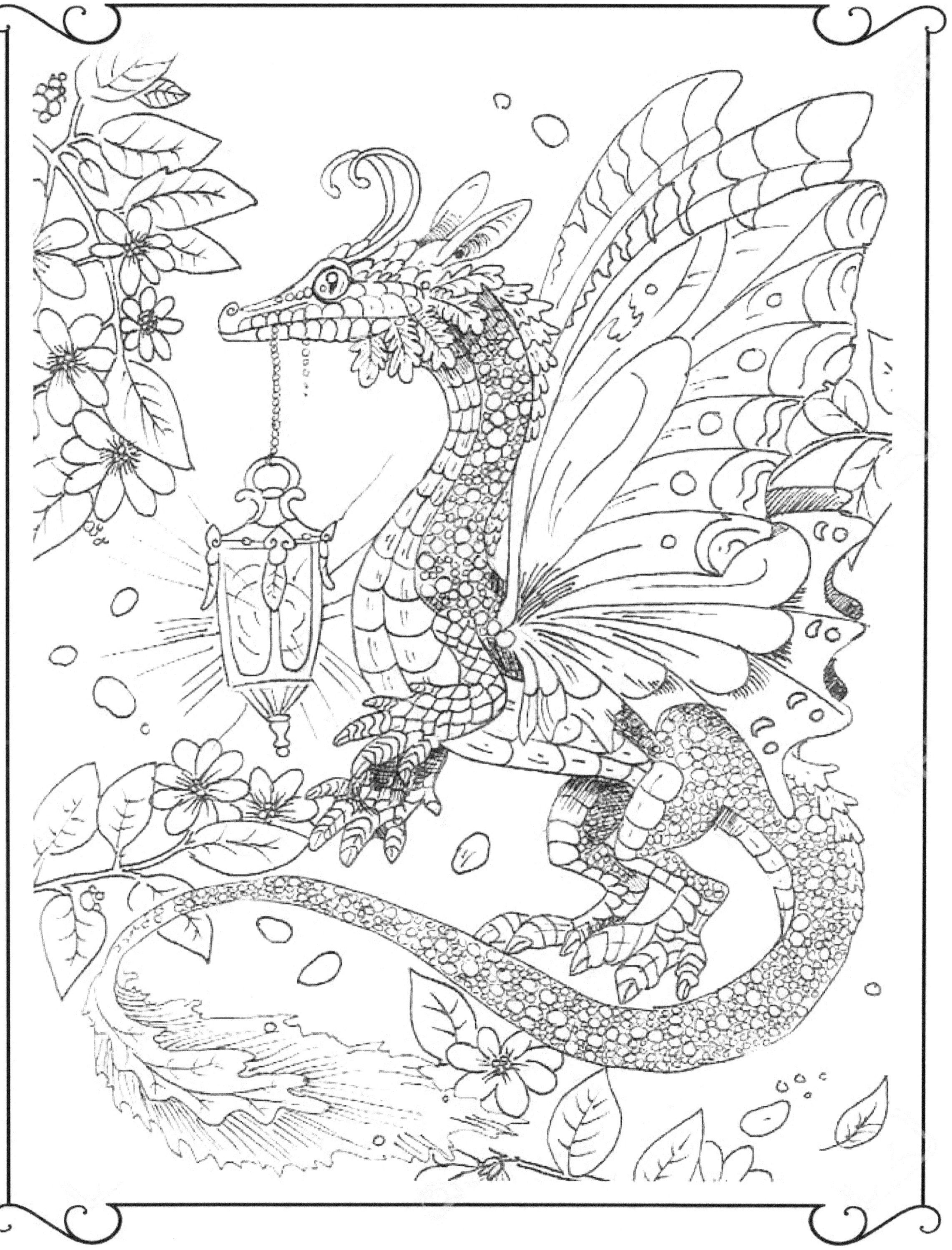

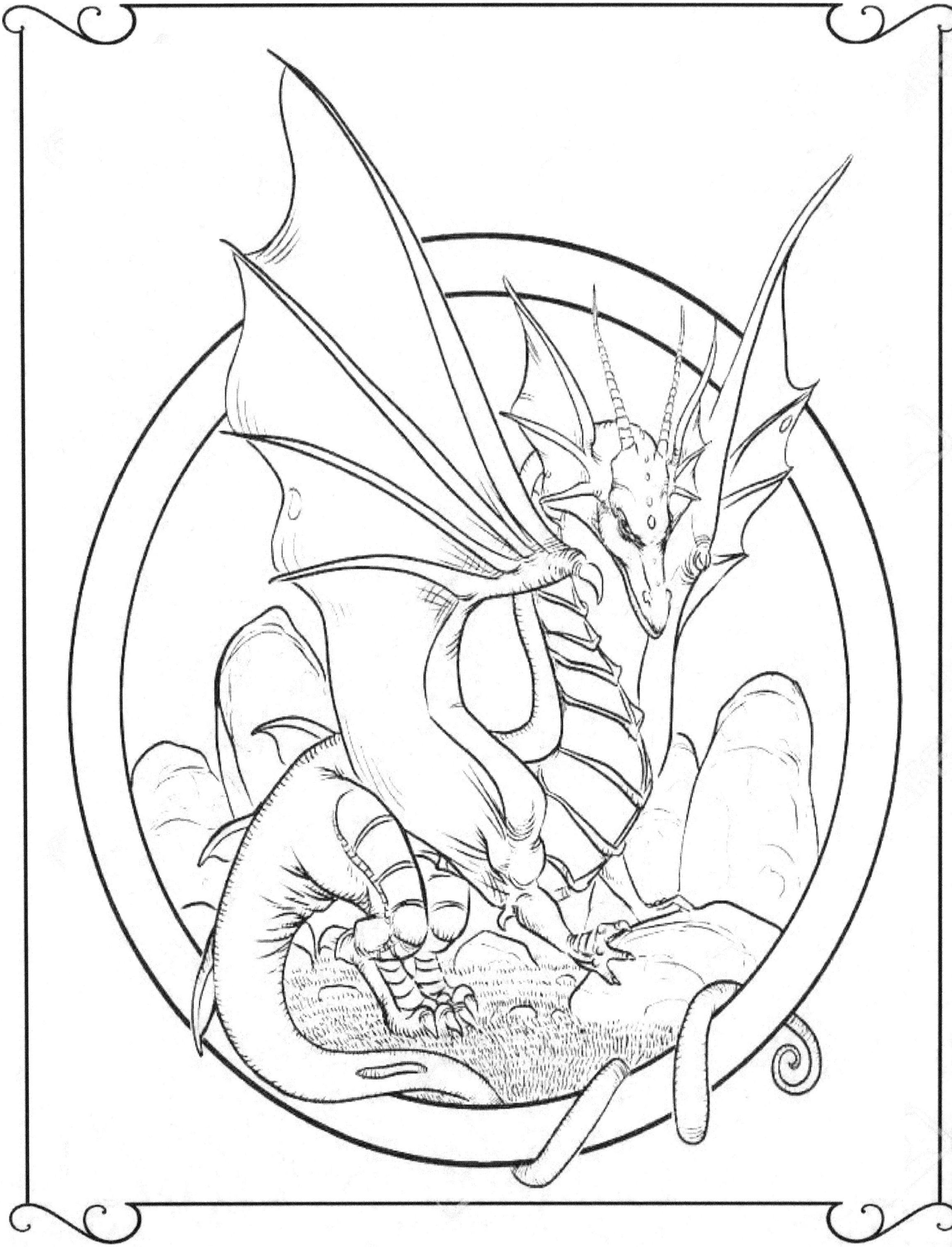

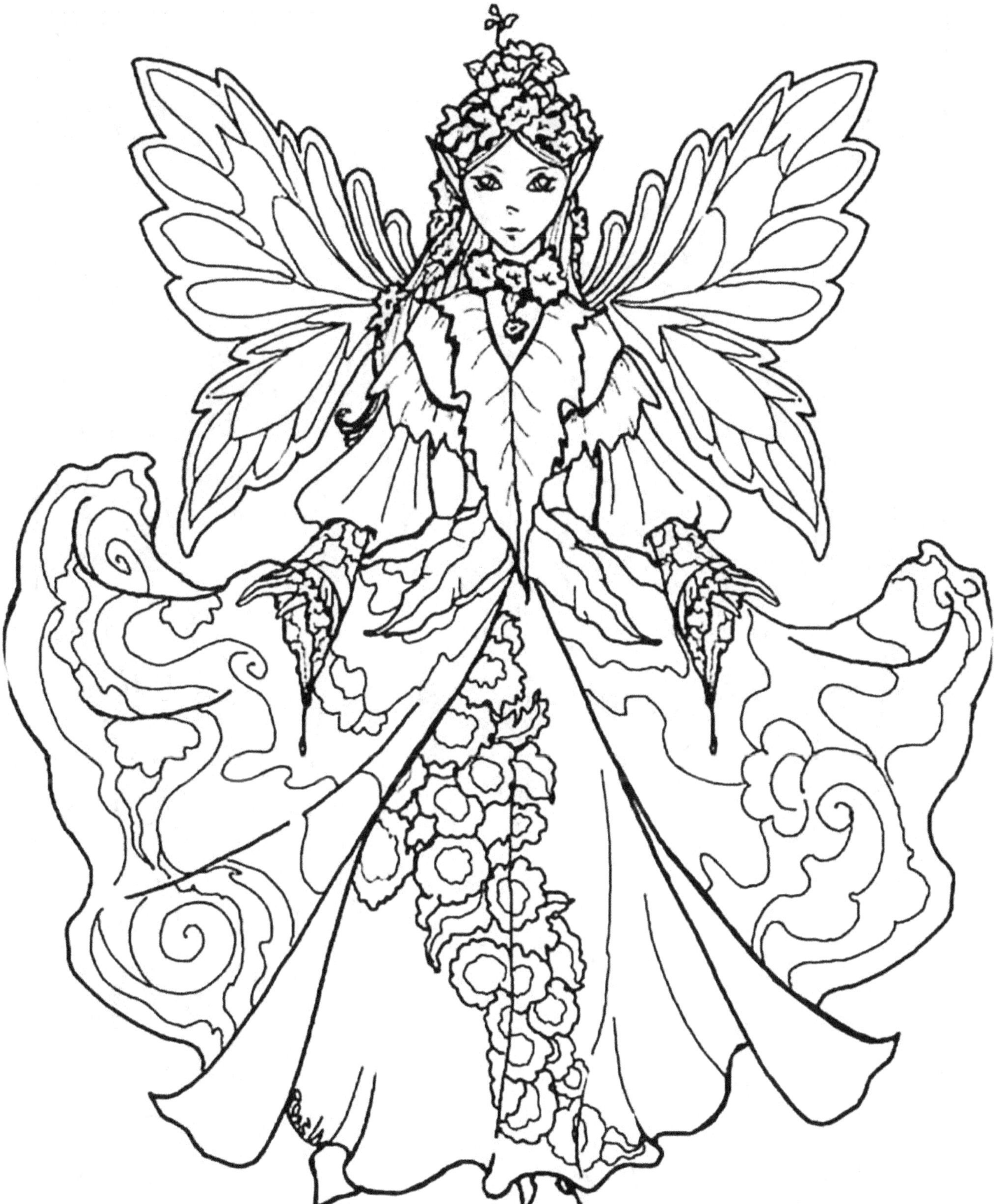

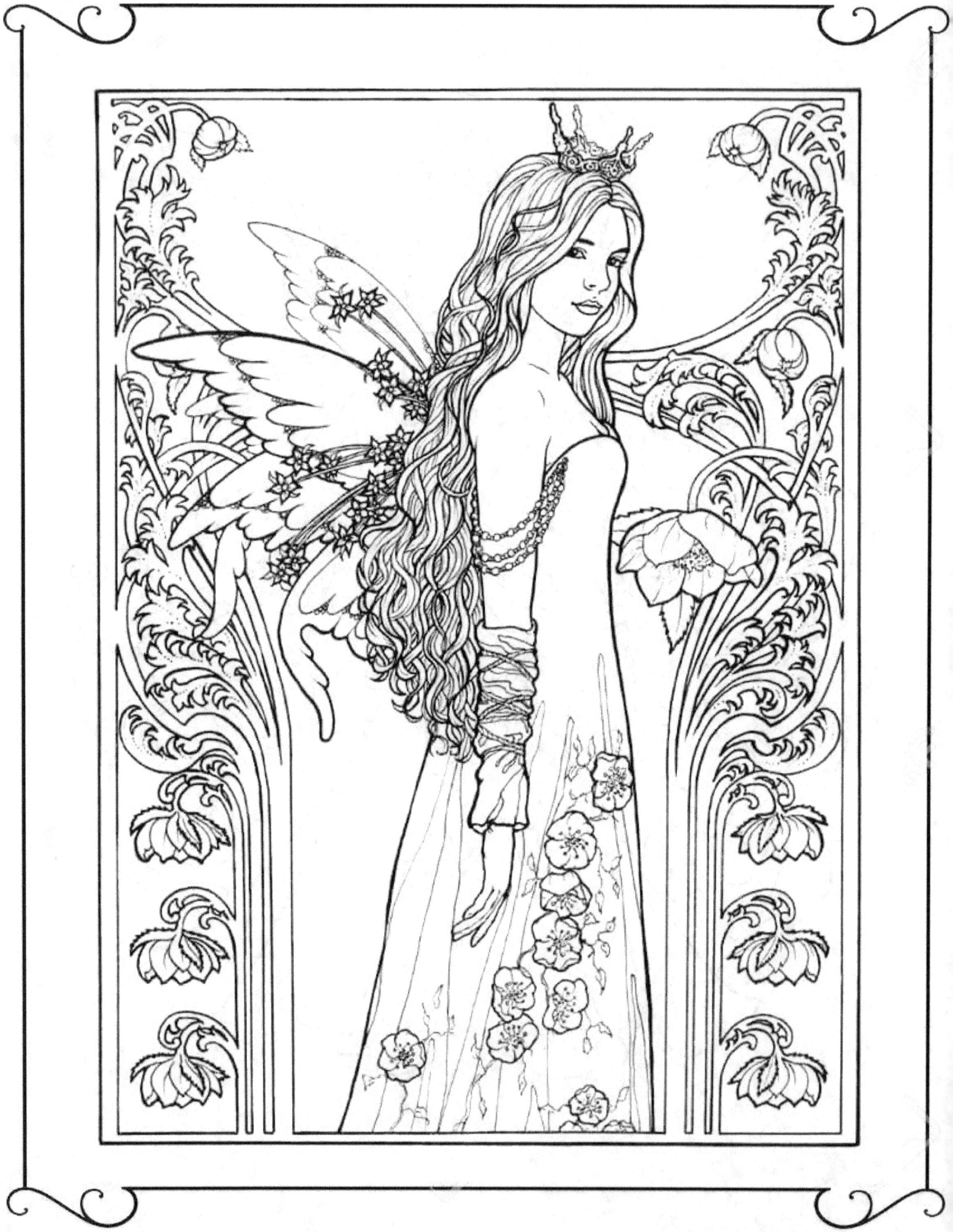

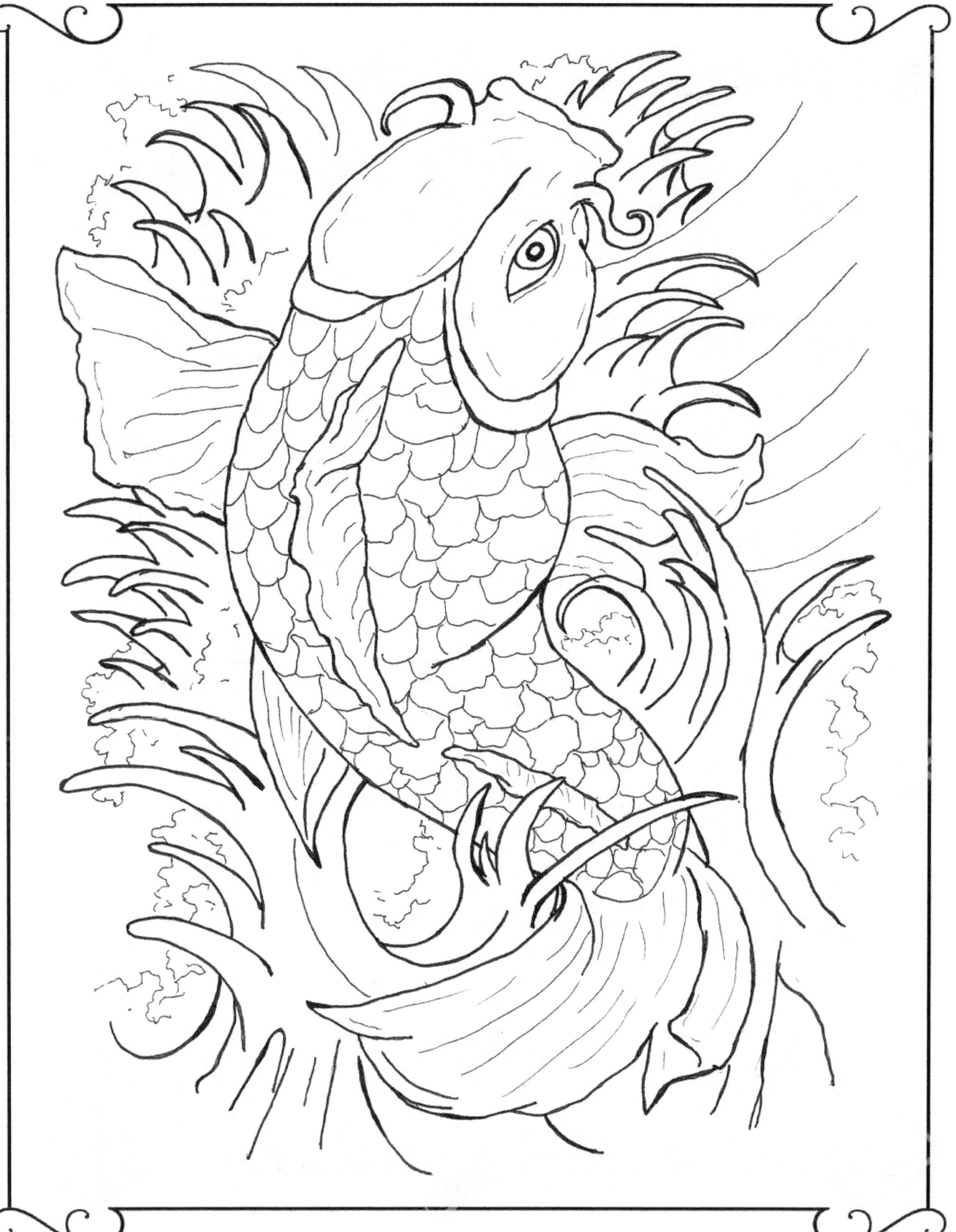

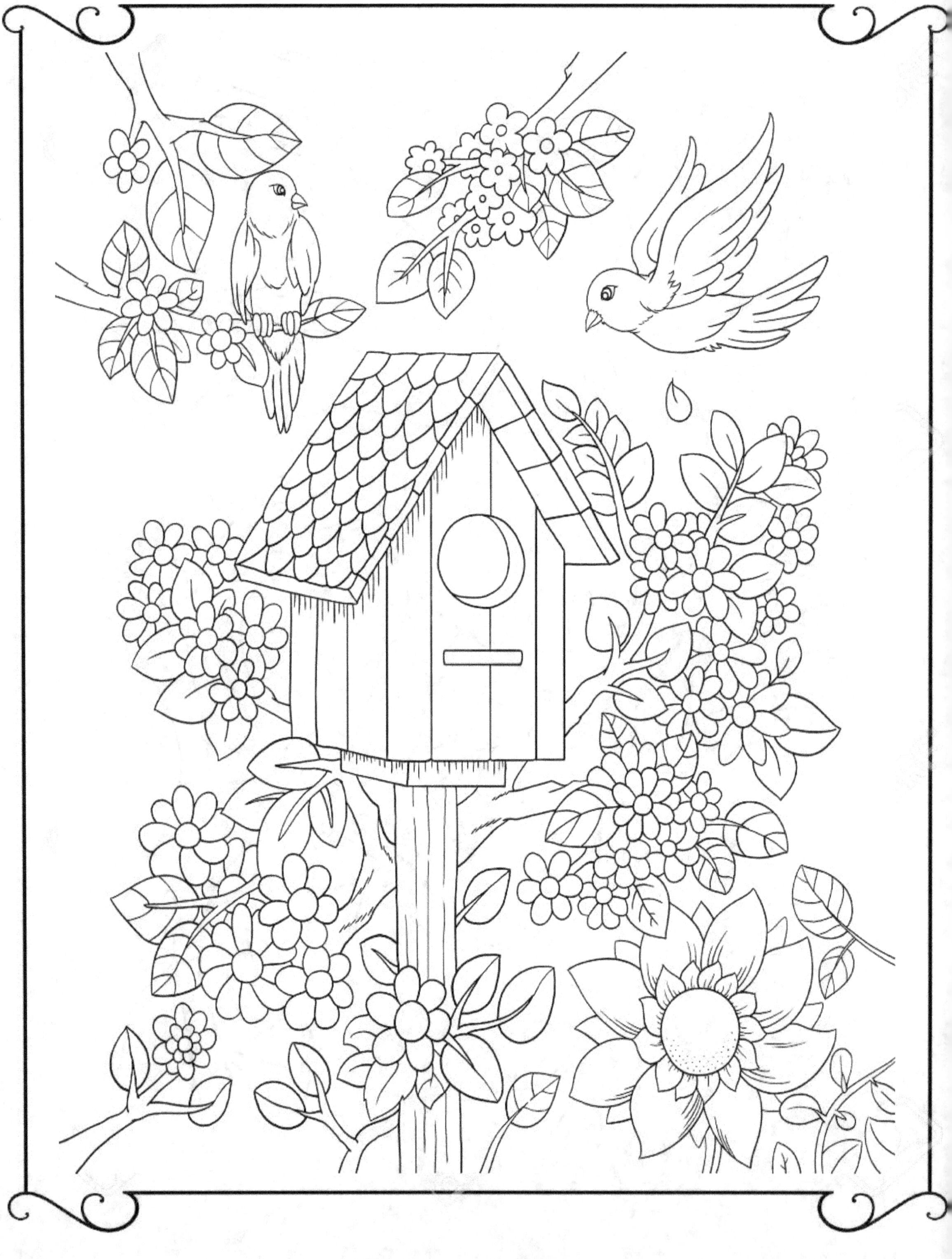

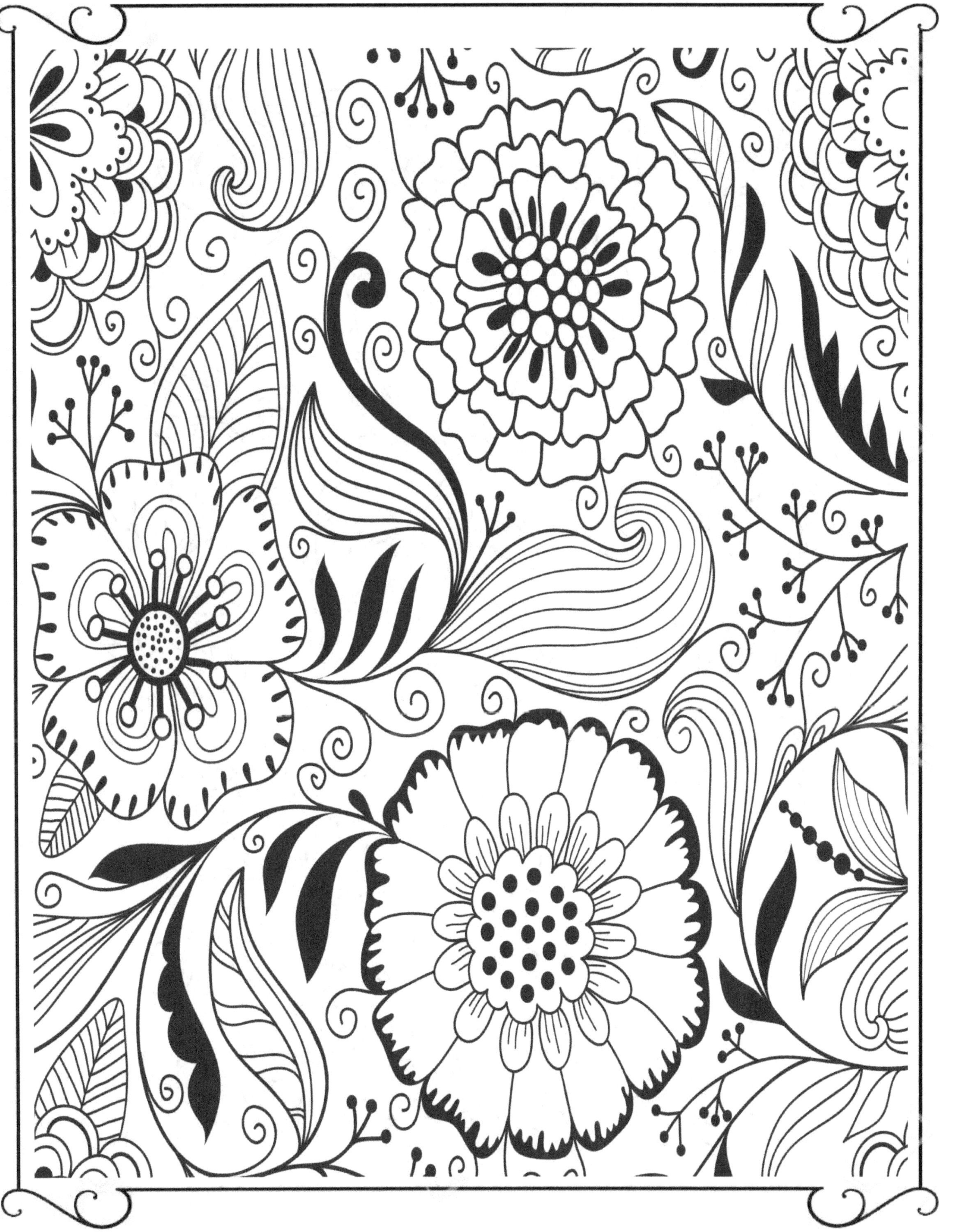

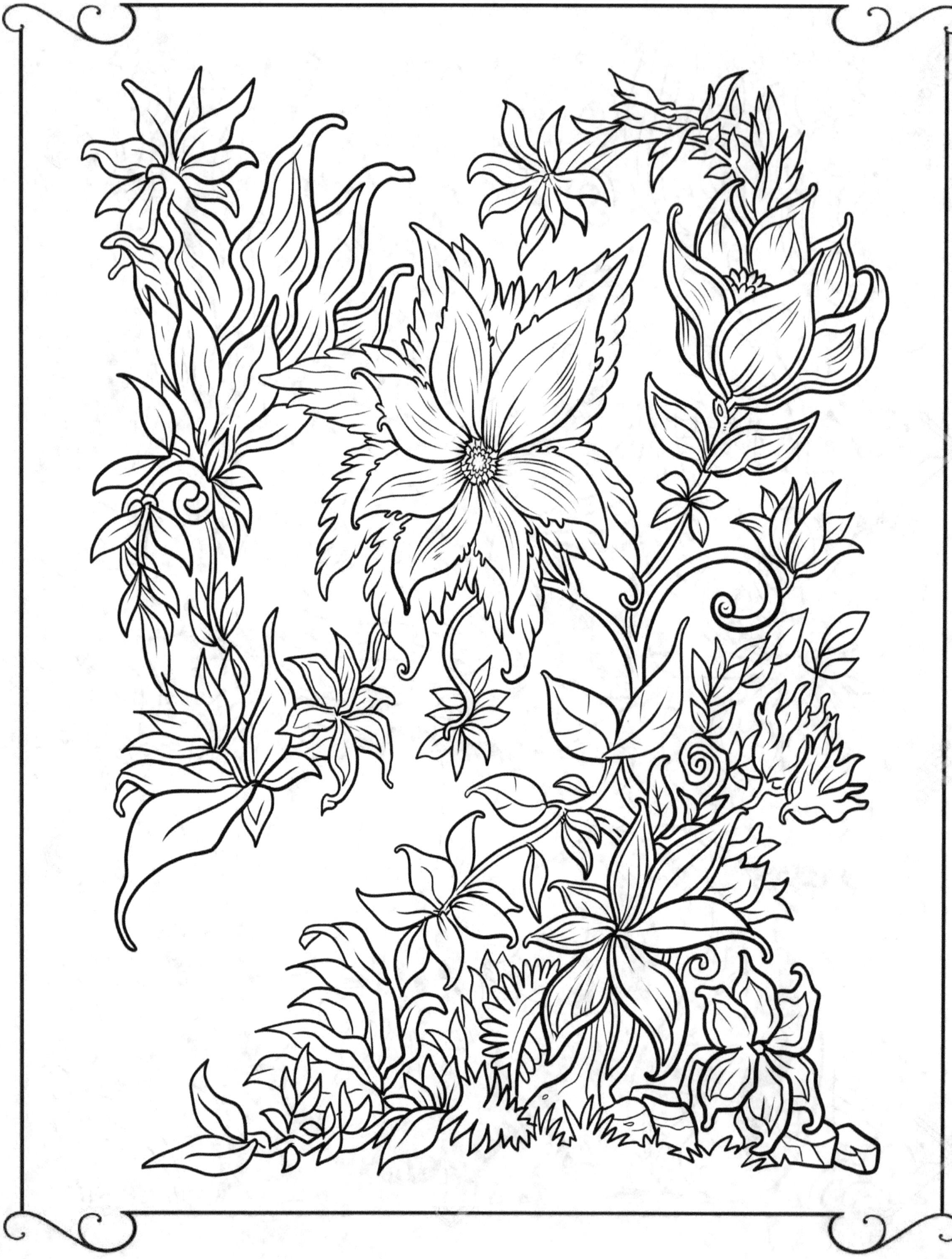

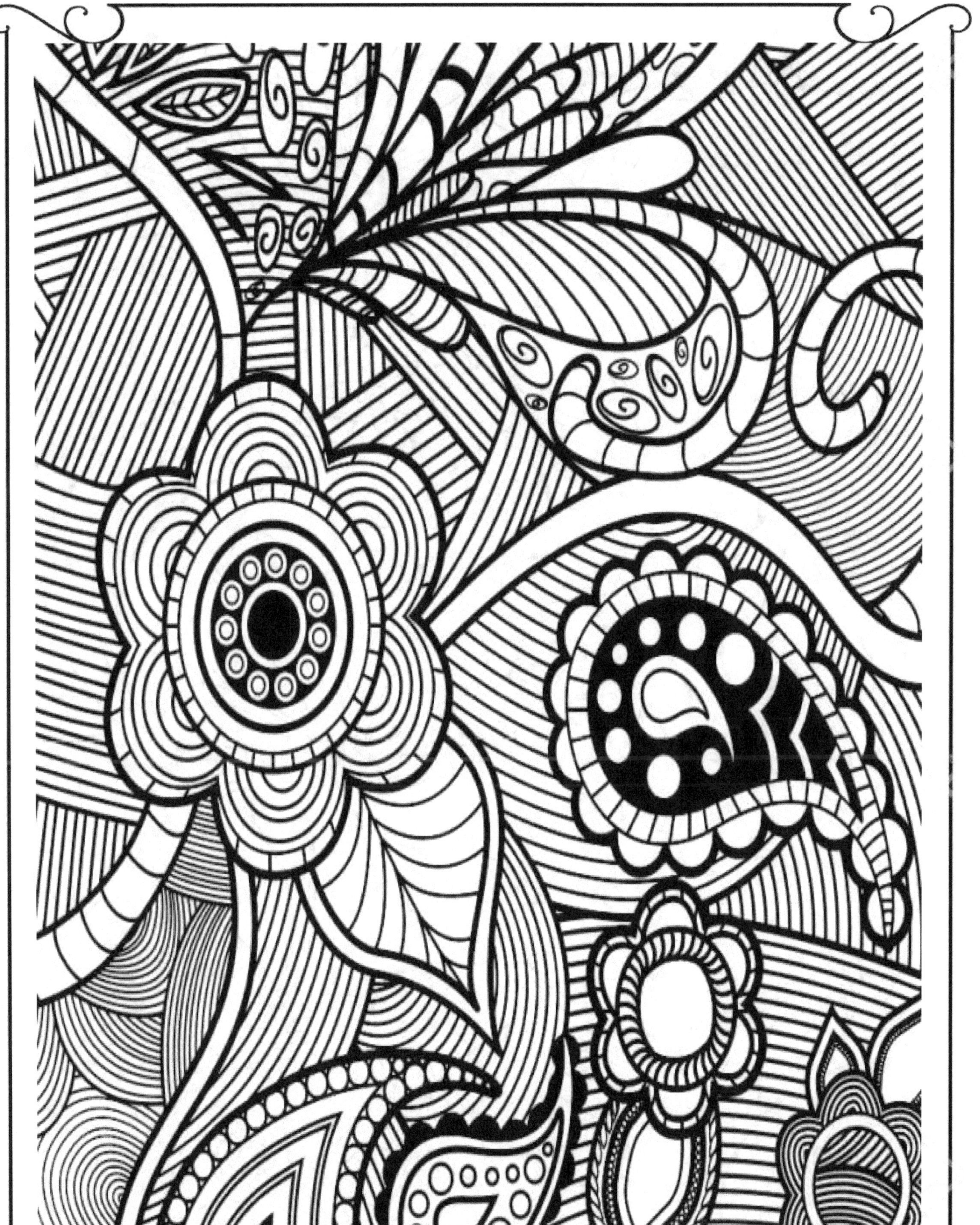

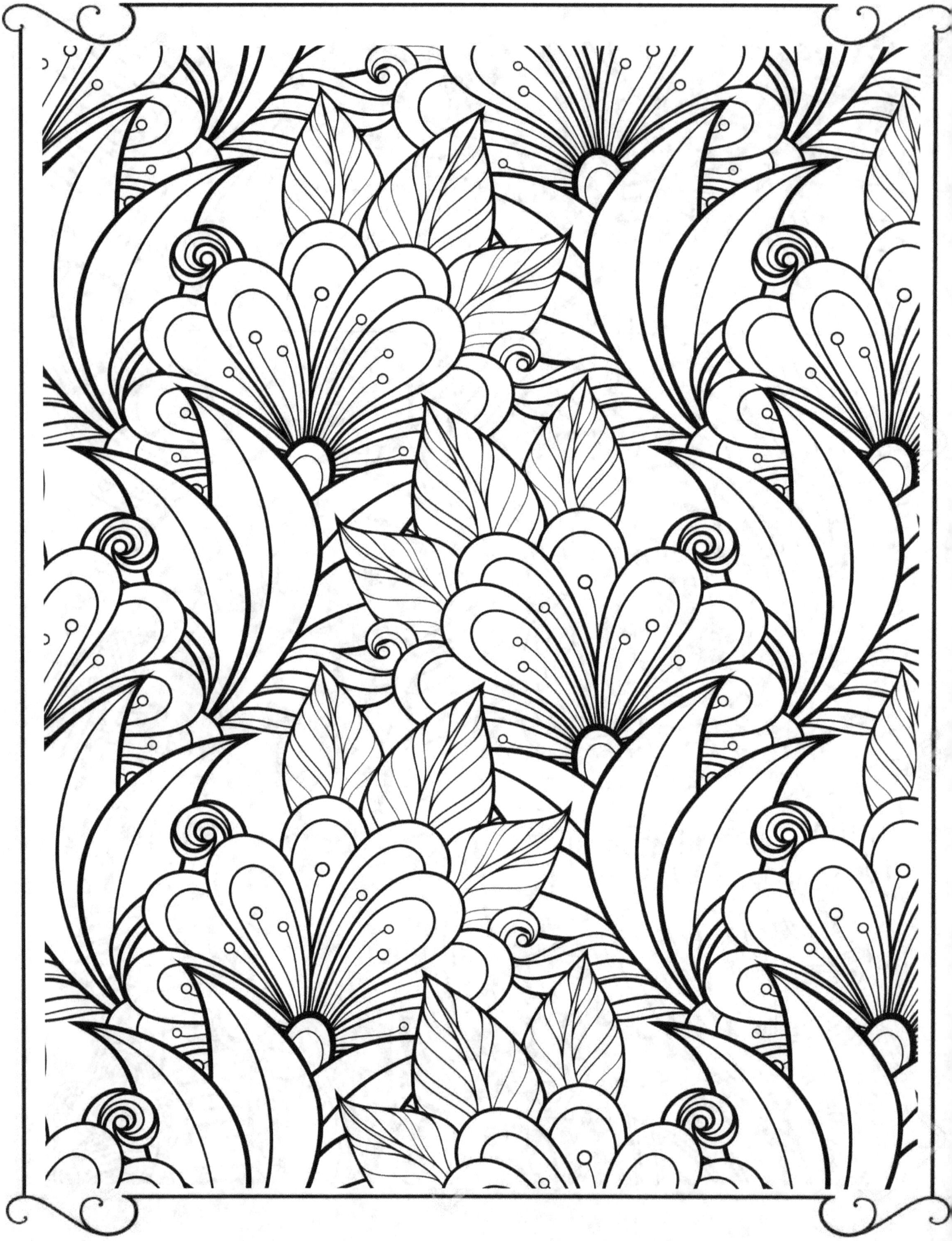

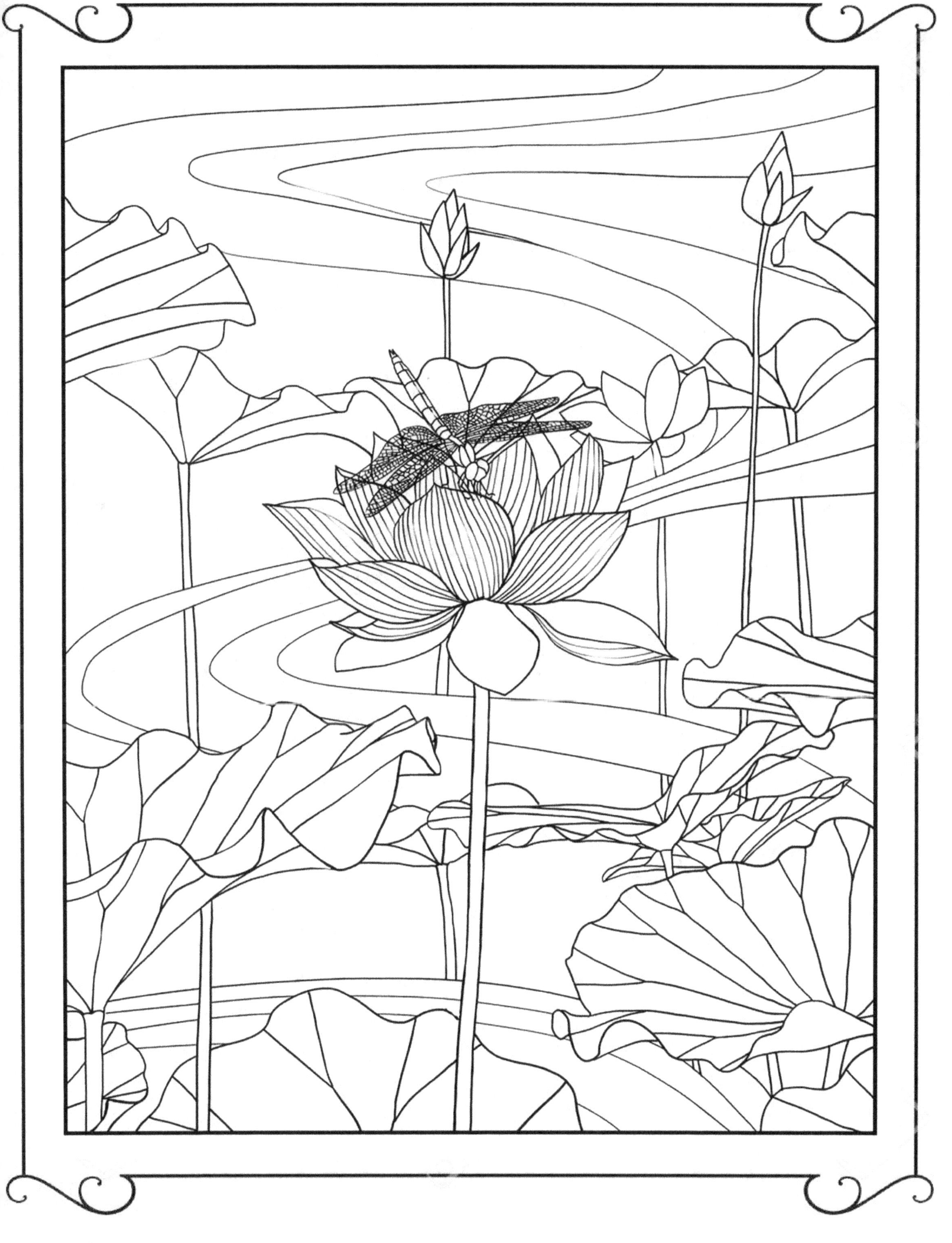

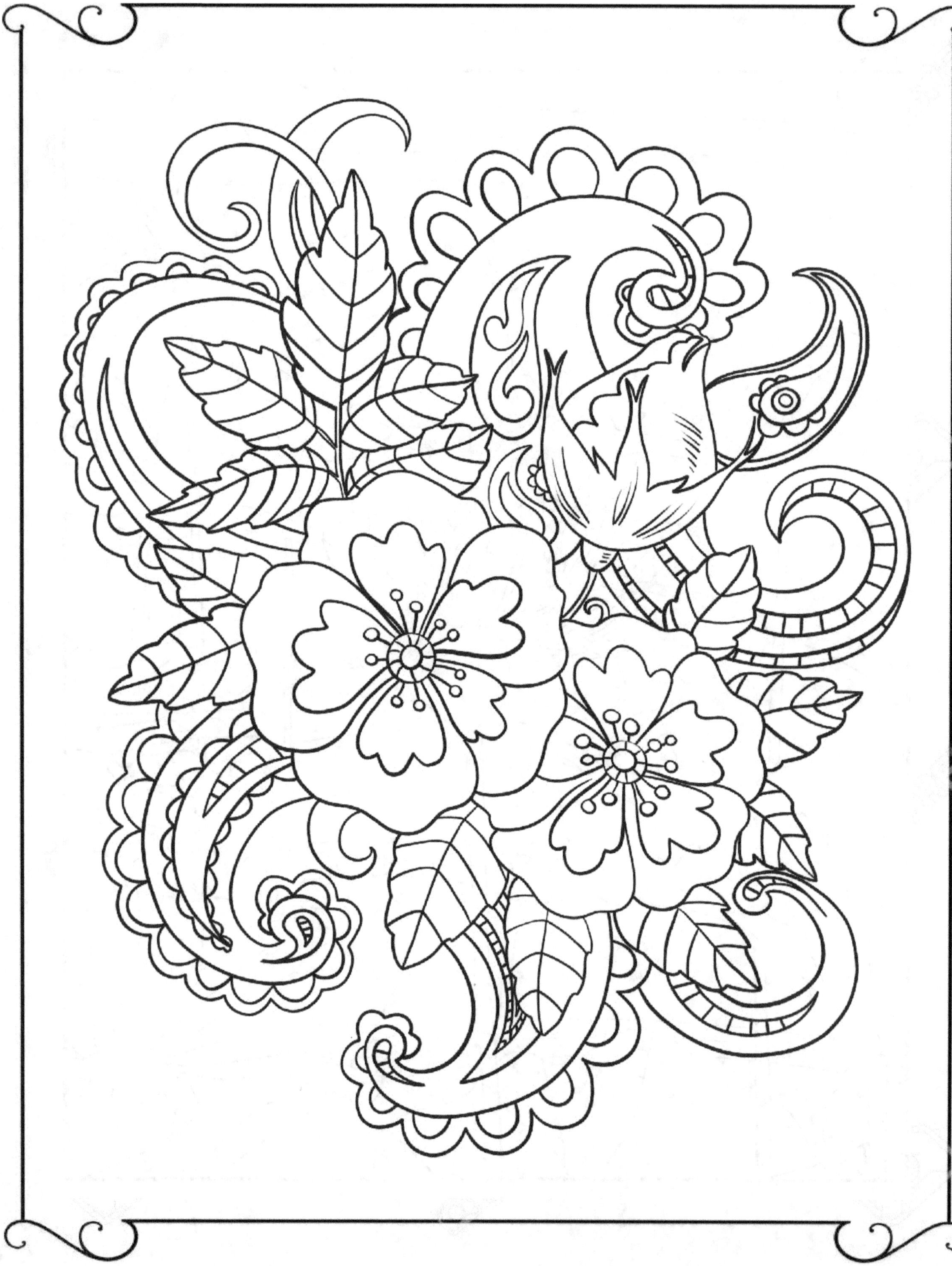

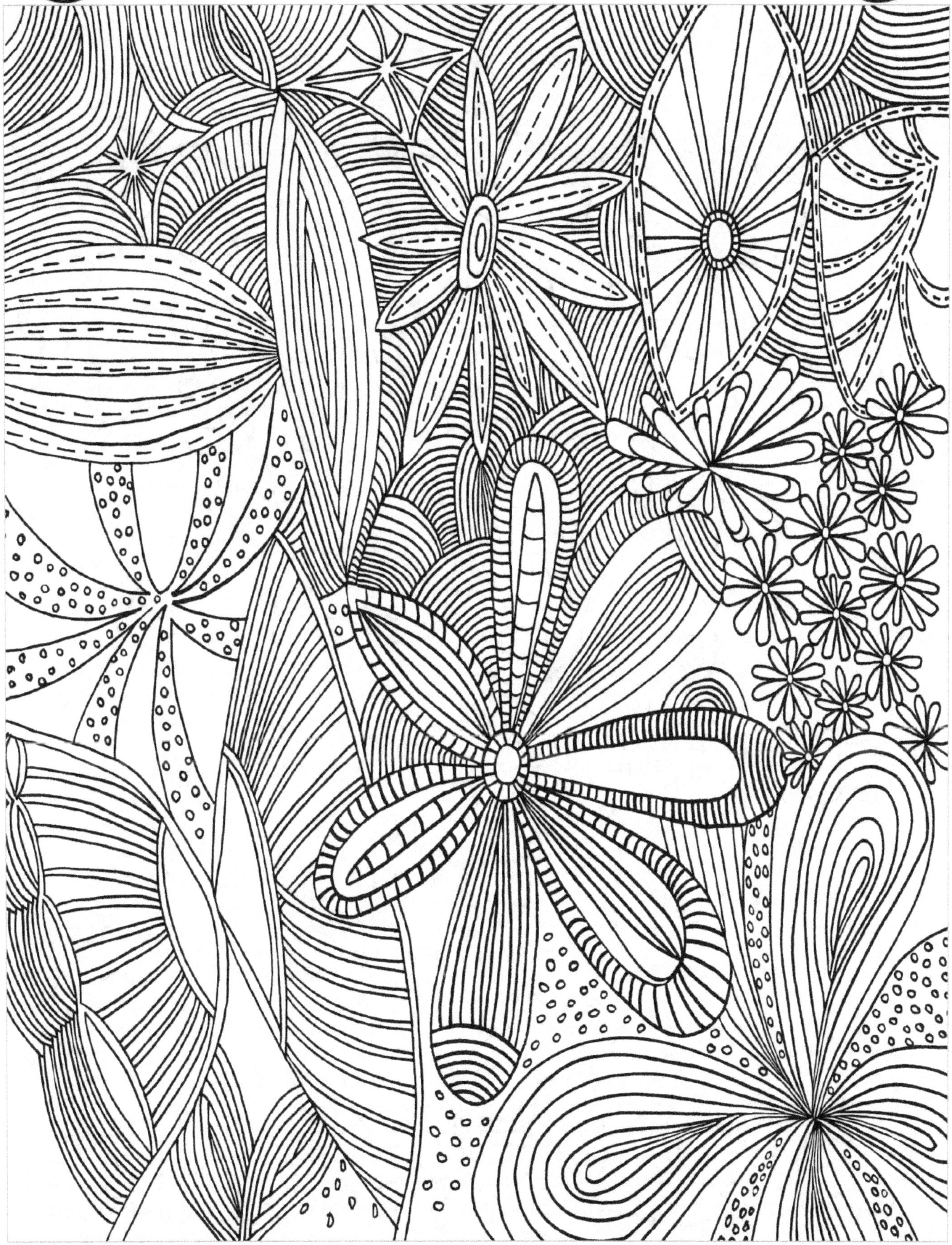

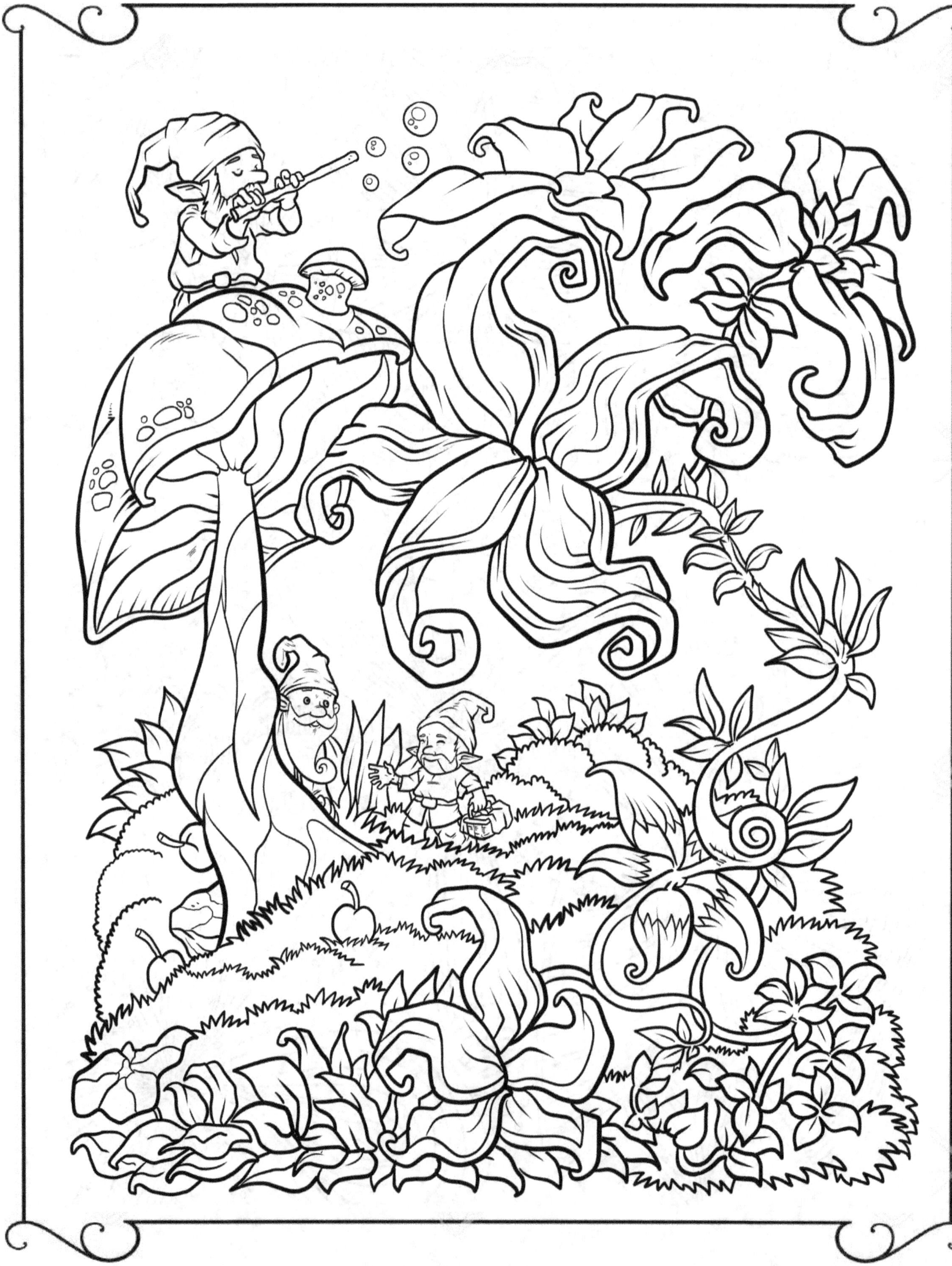

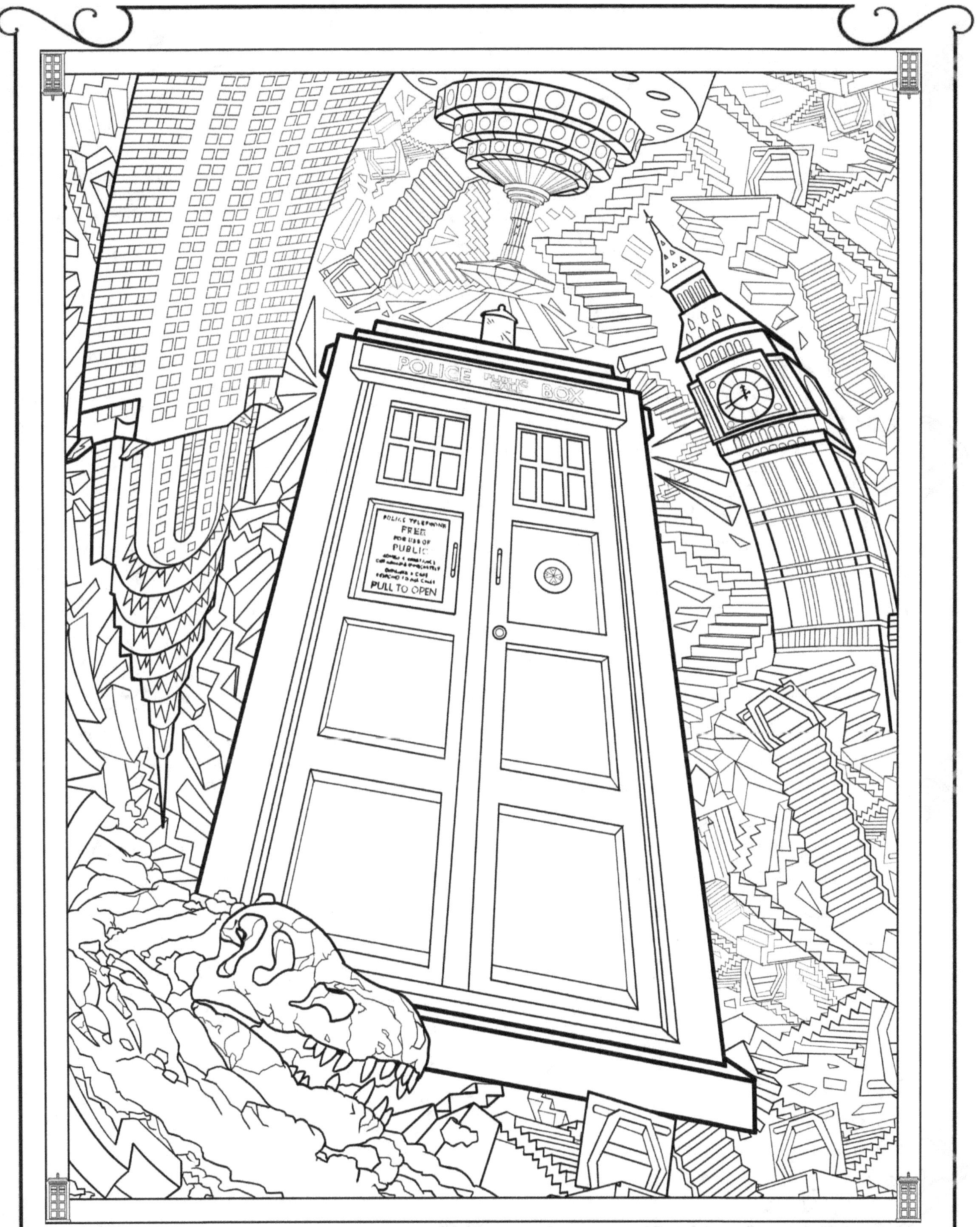
POLICE PUBLIC CALL BOX
POLICE TELEPHONE
FREE
FOR USE OF
PUBLIC
PULL TO OPEN

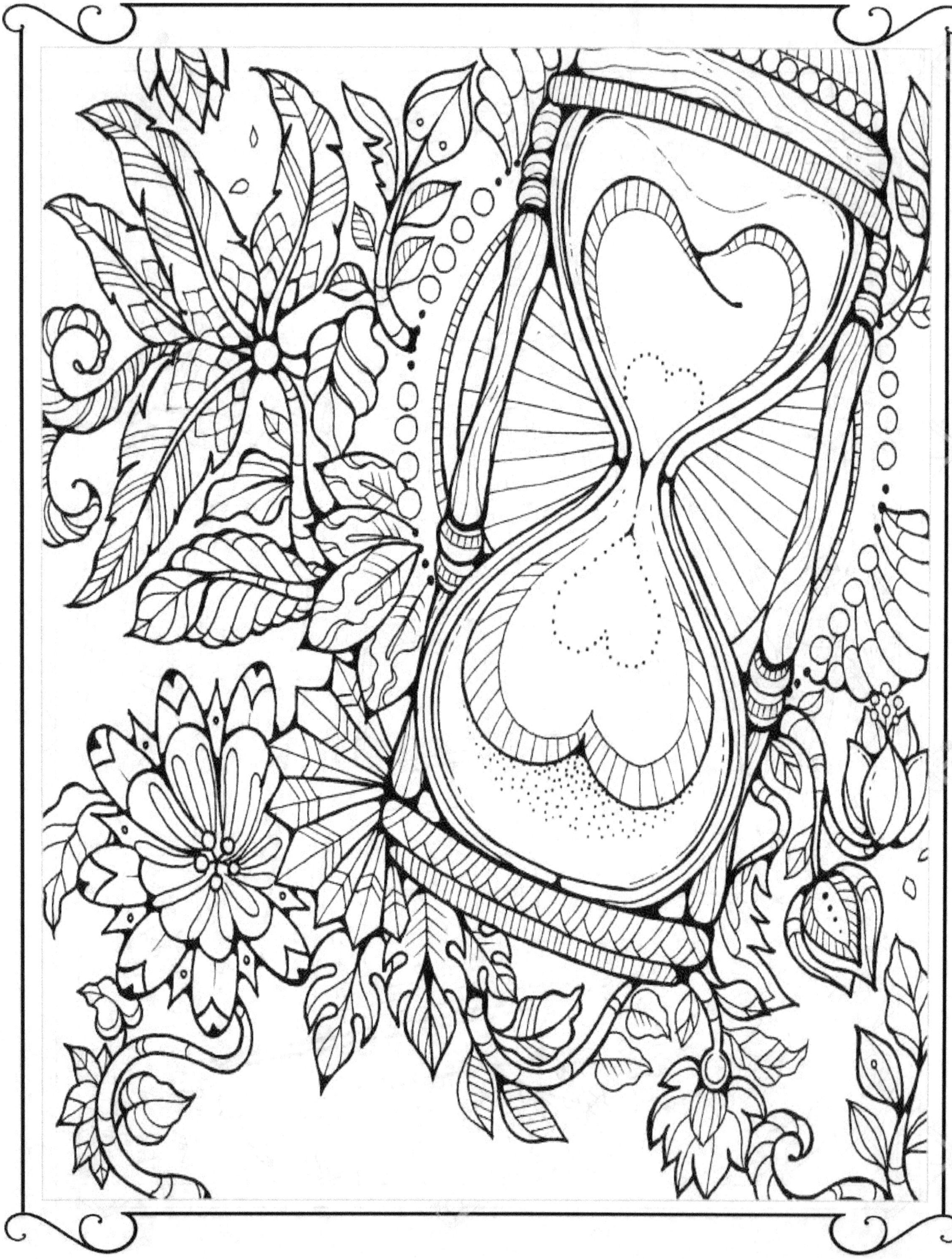

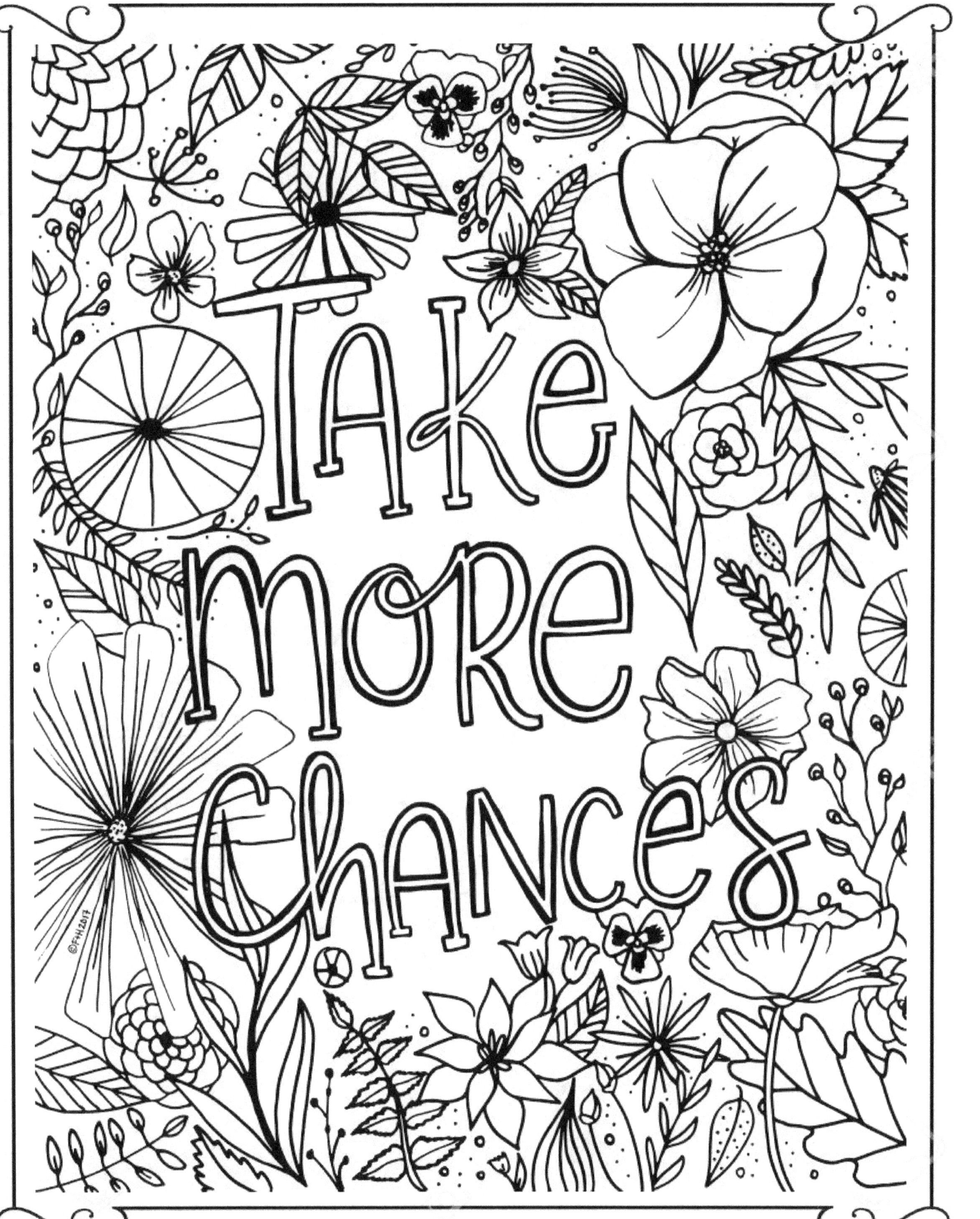
Take
more
Chances

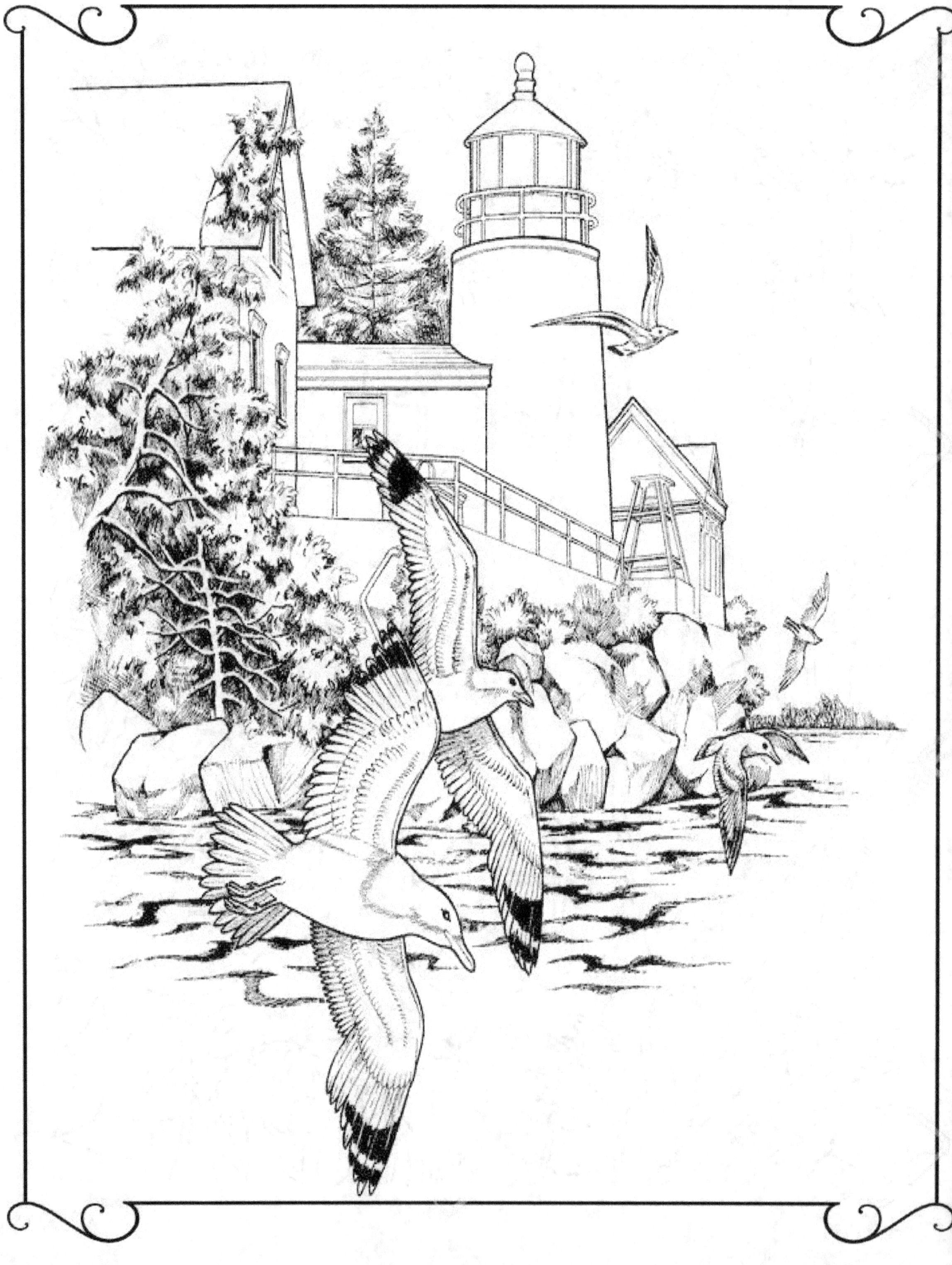

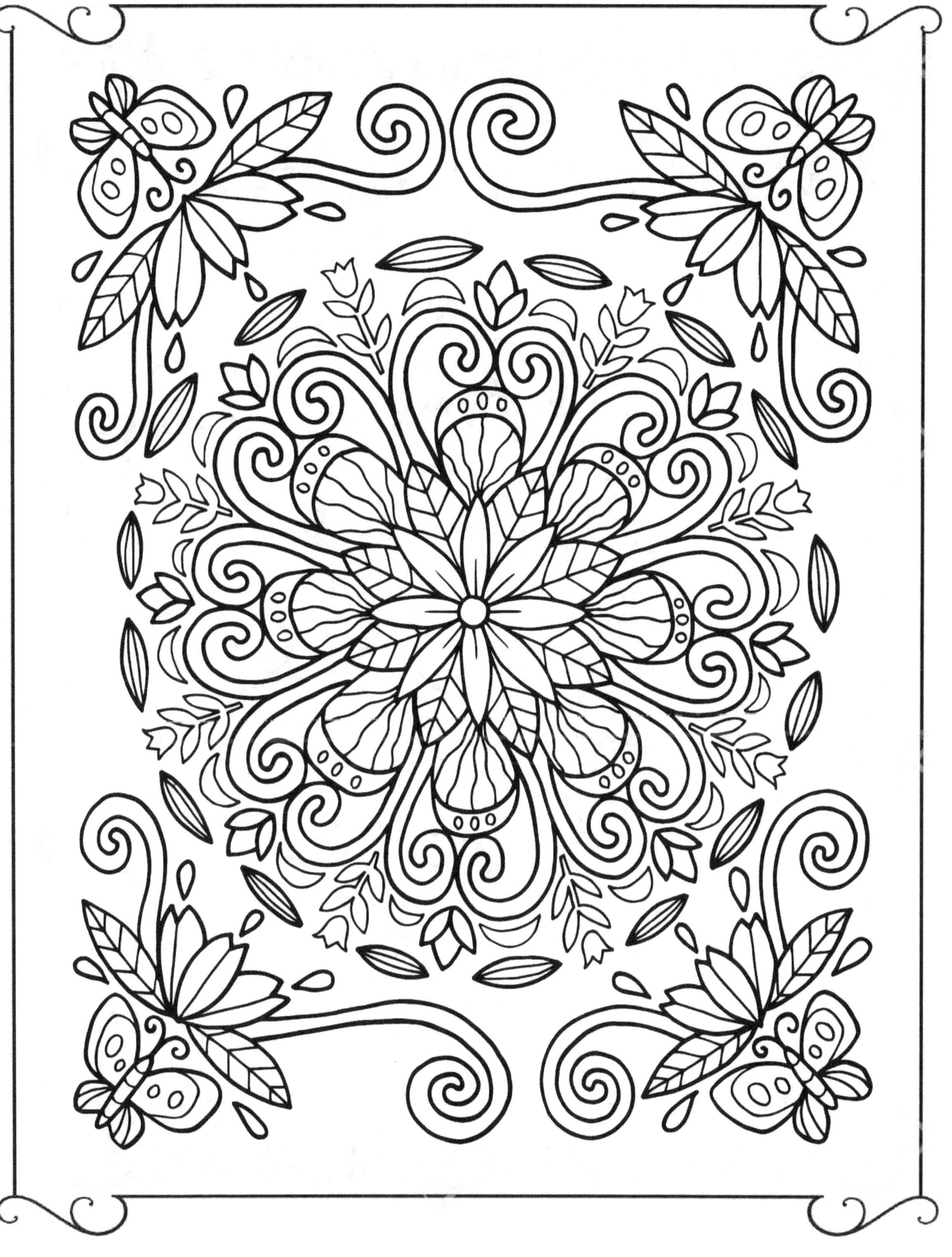

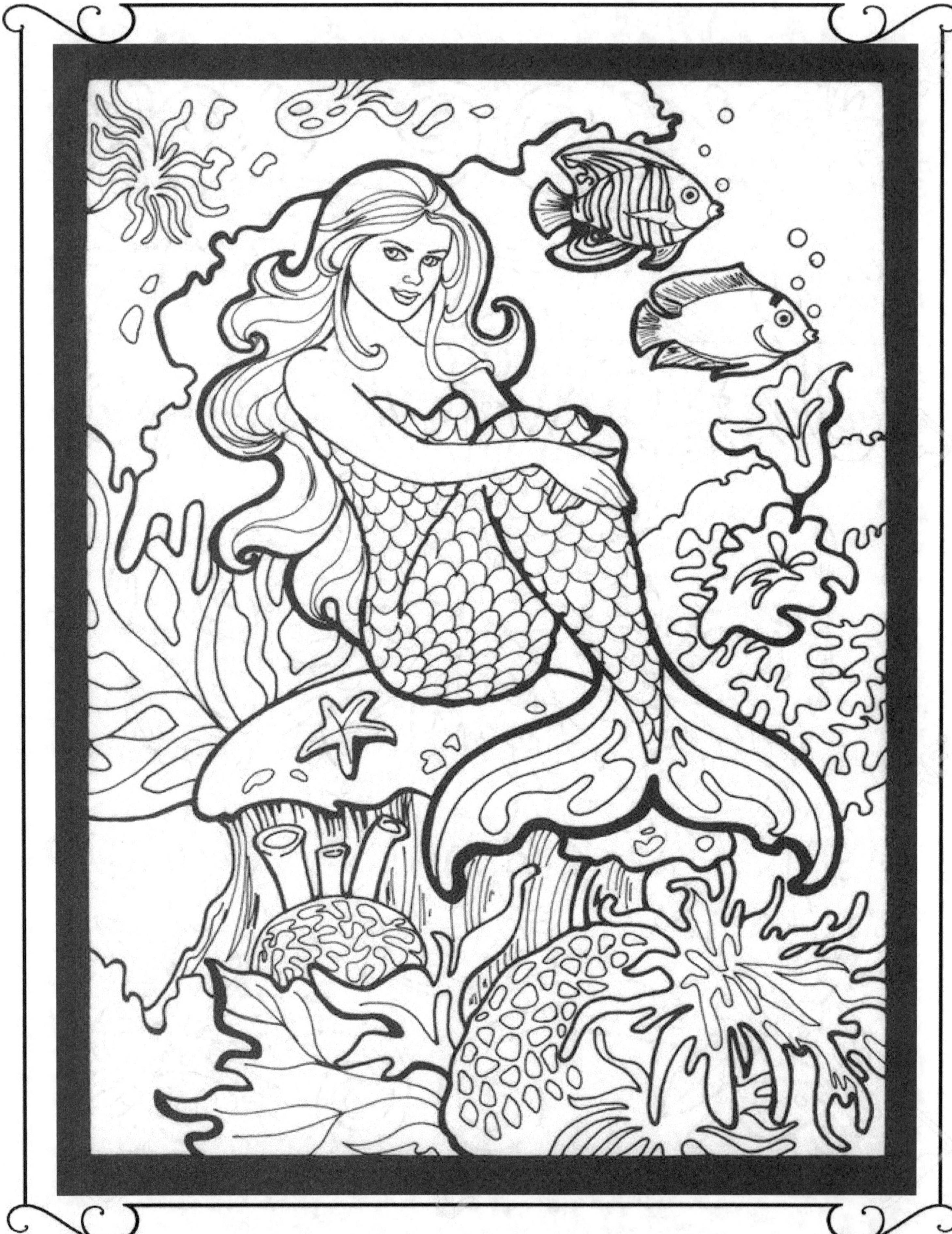

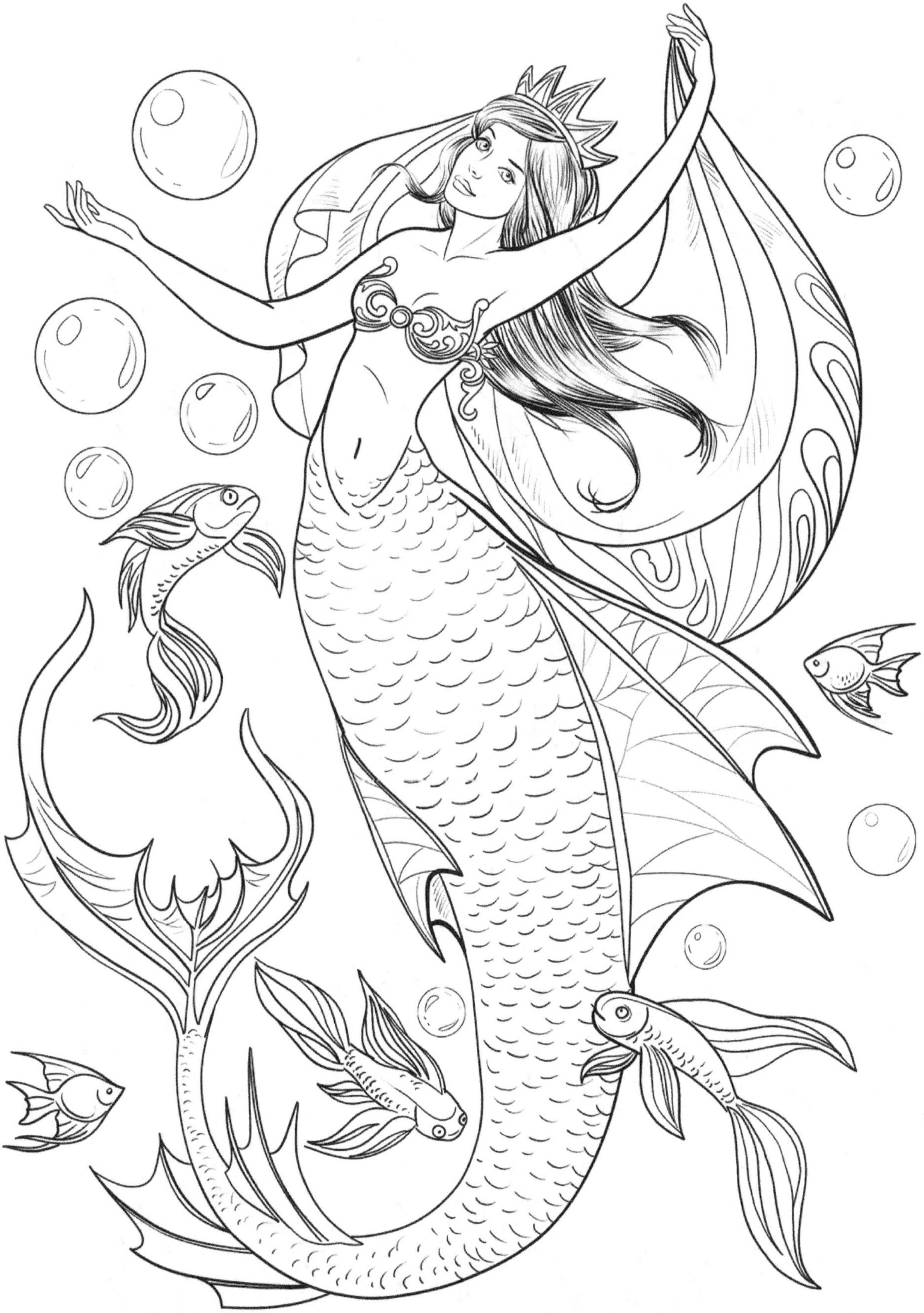

Petunia

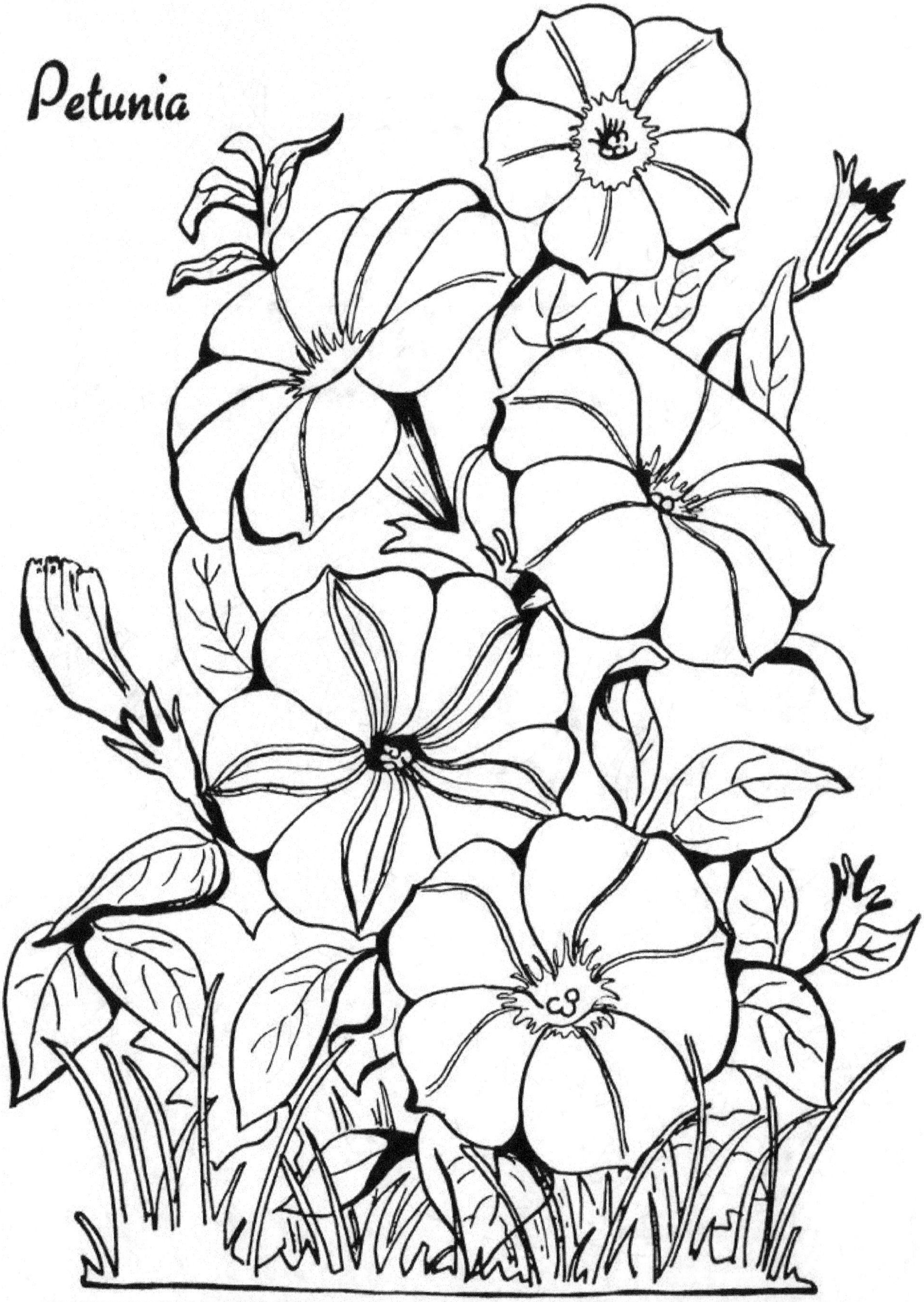

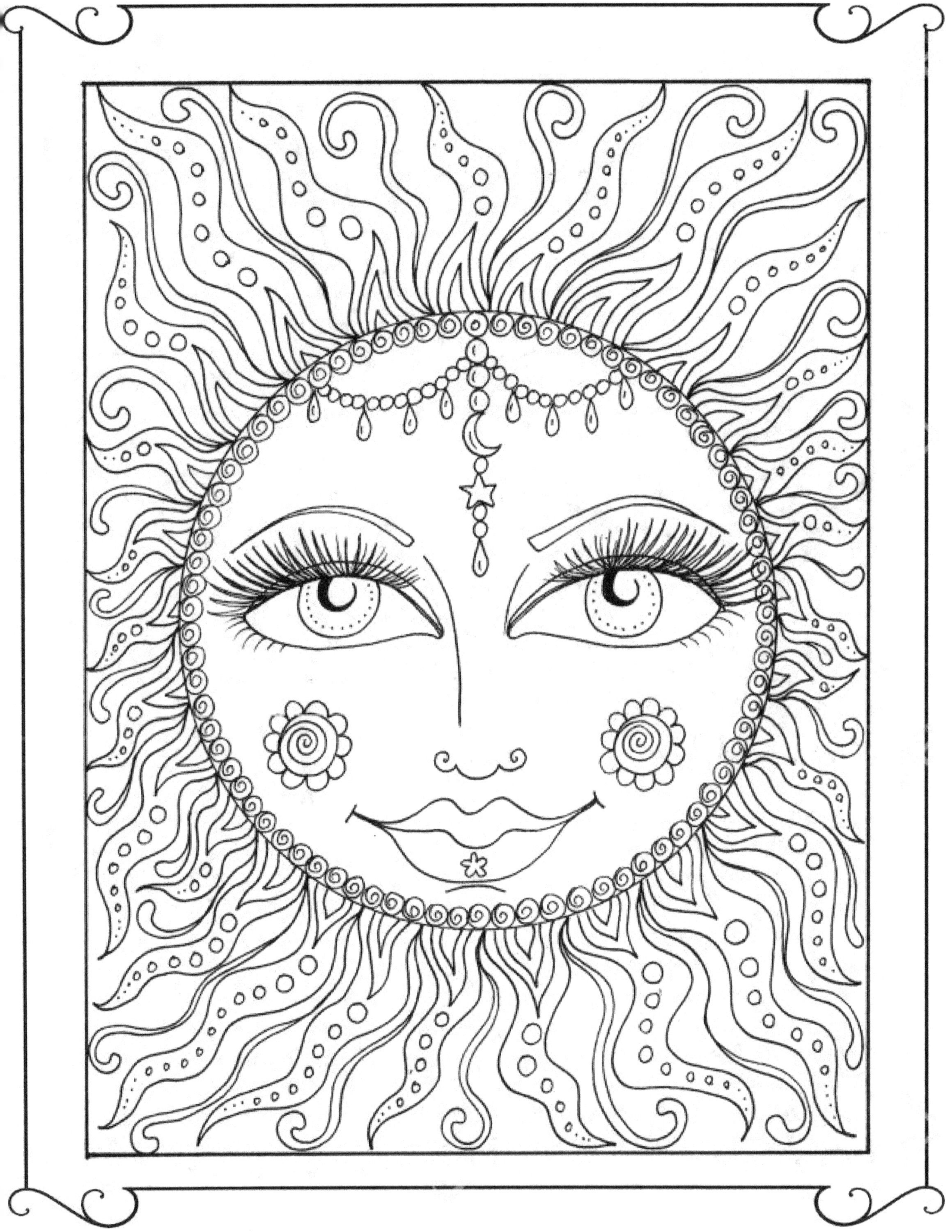

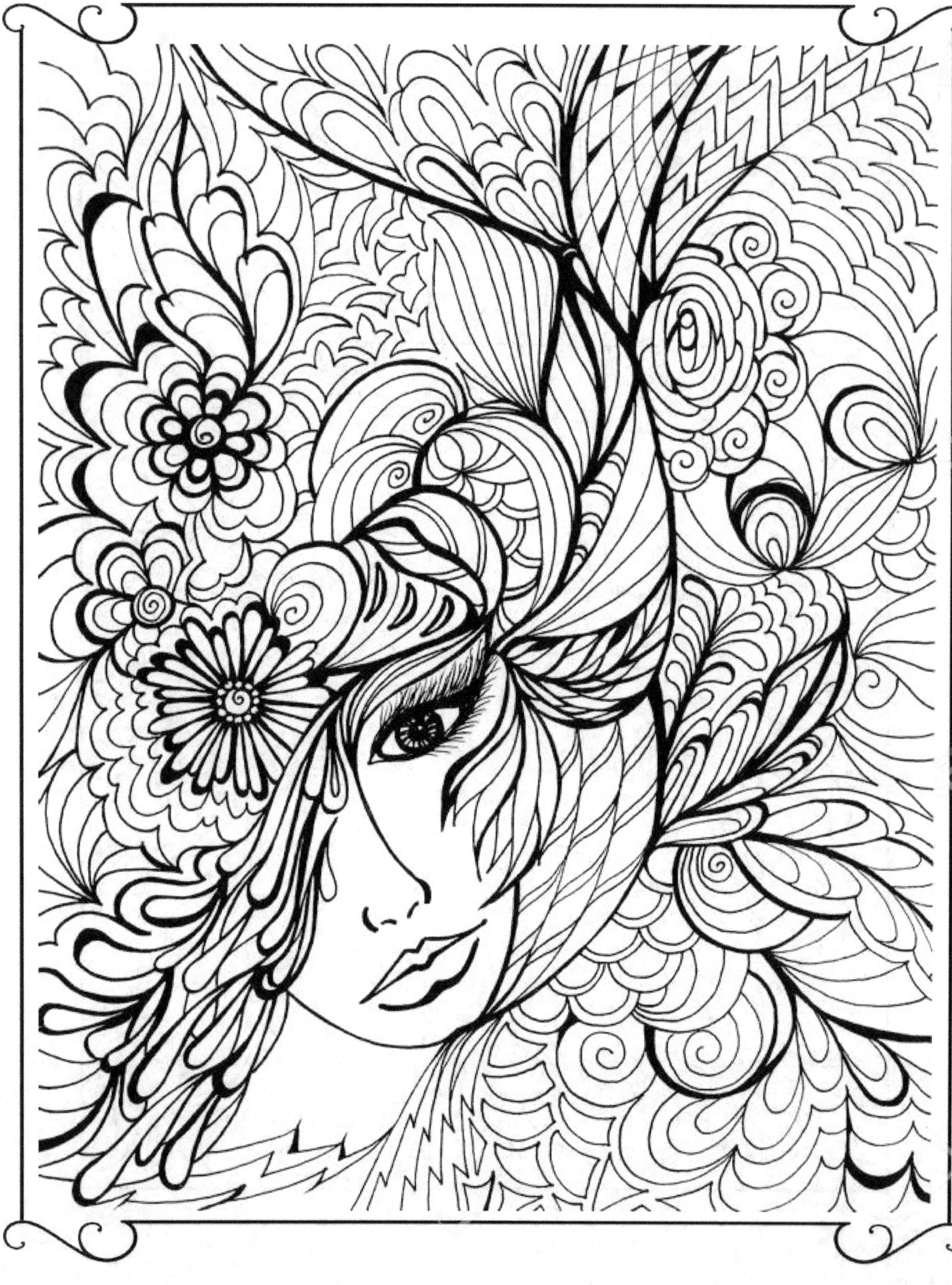

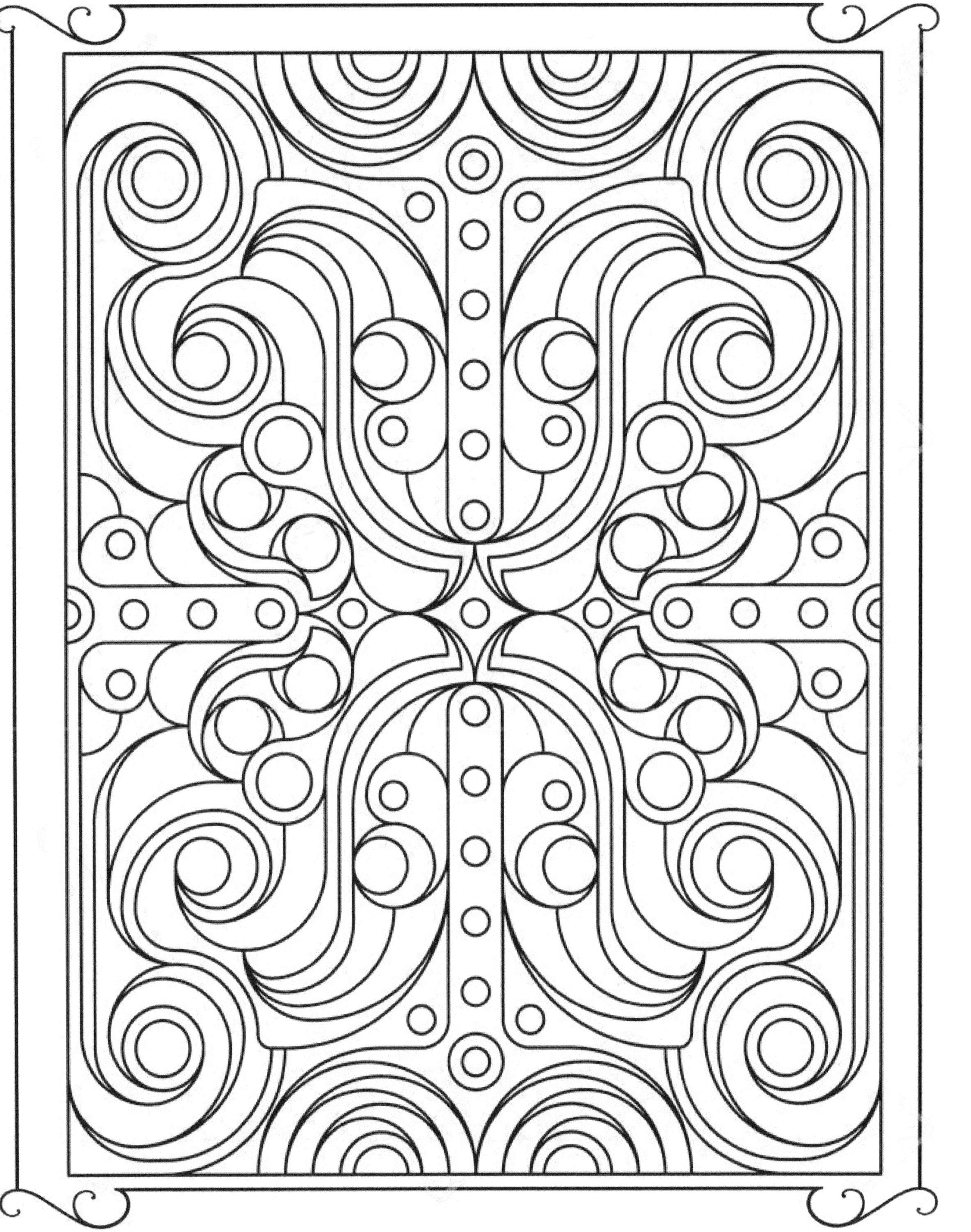

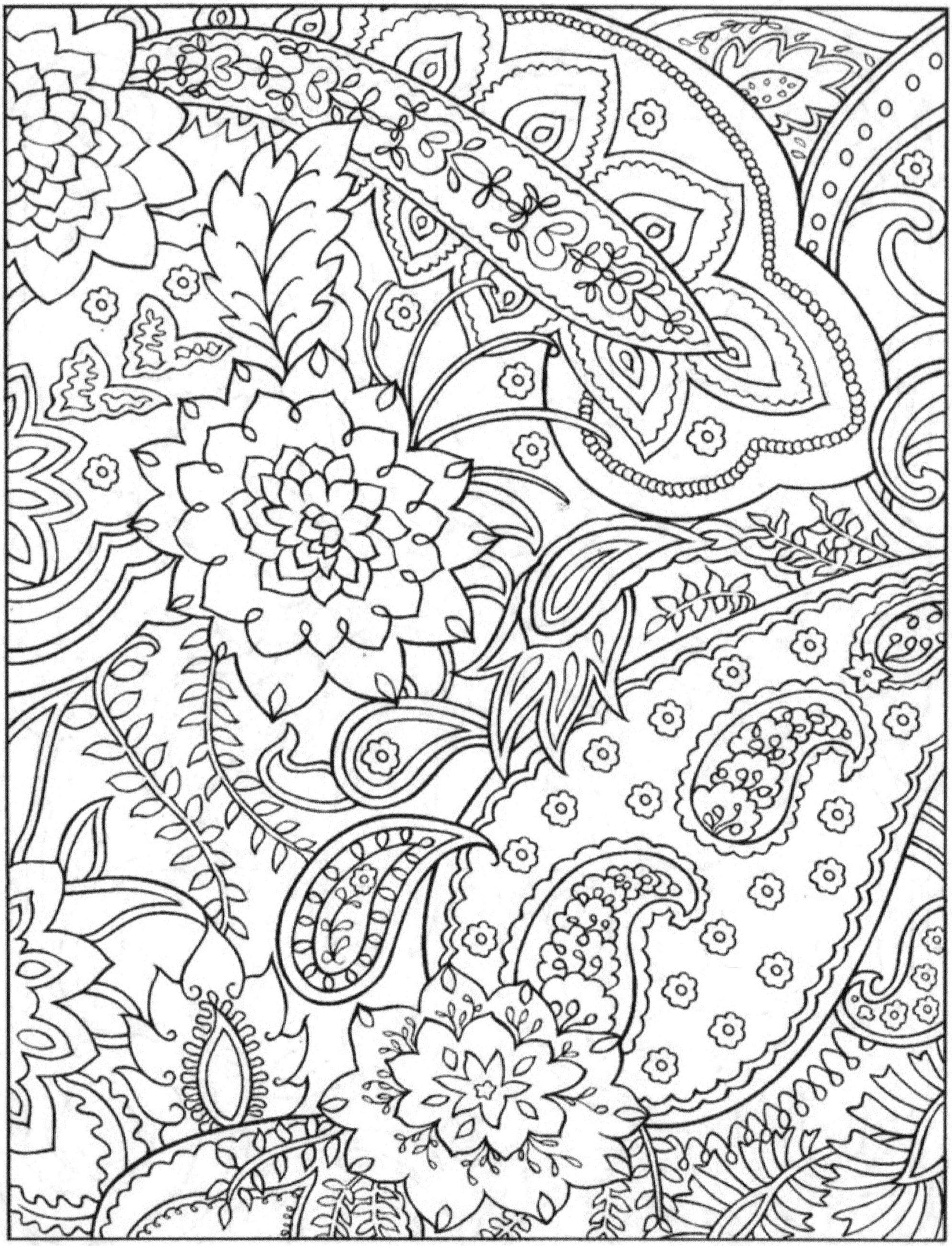

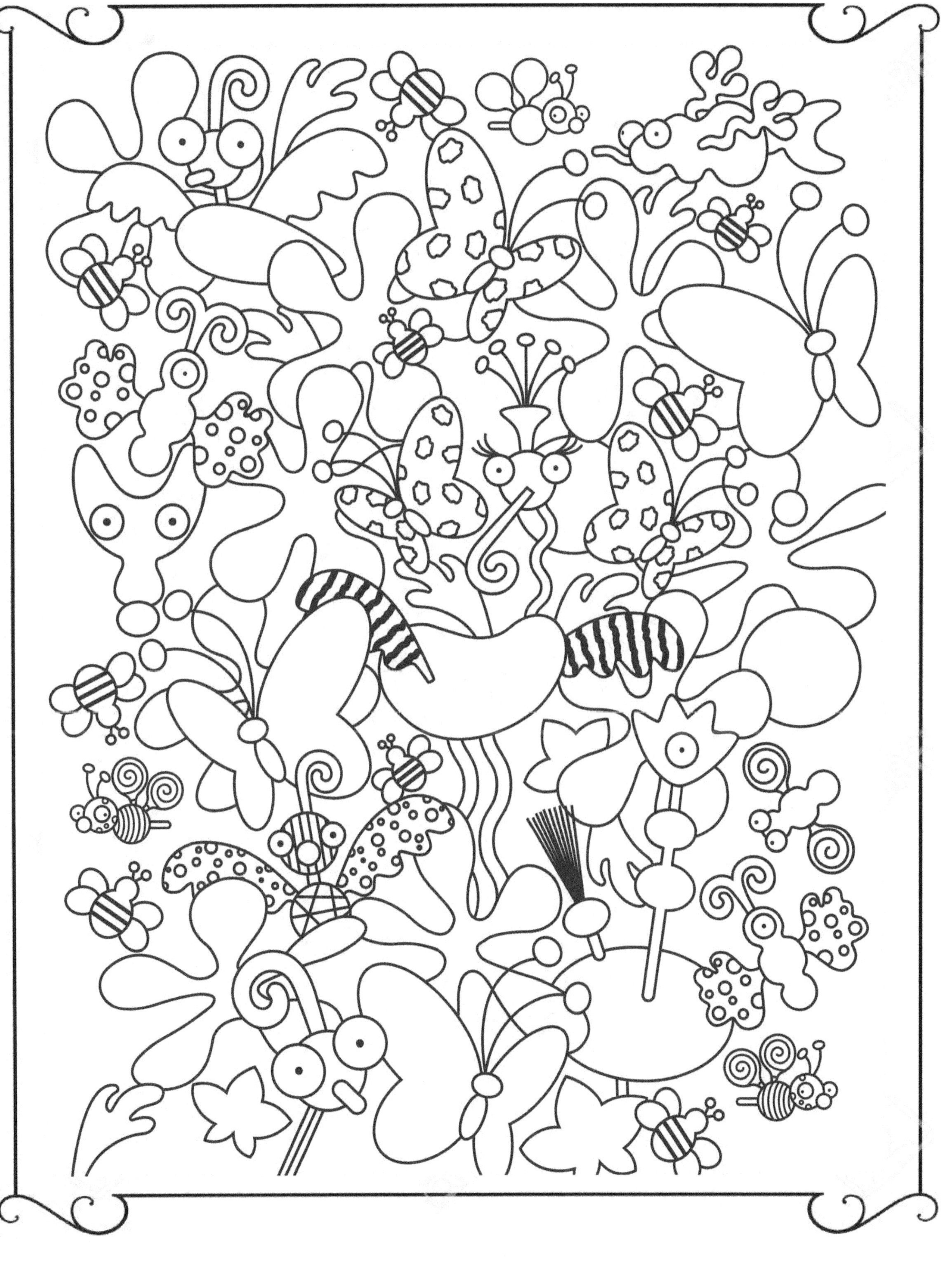

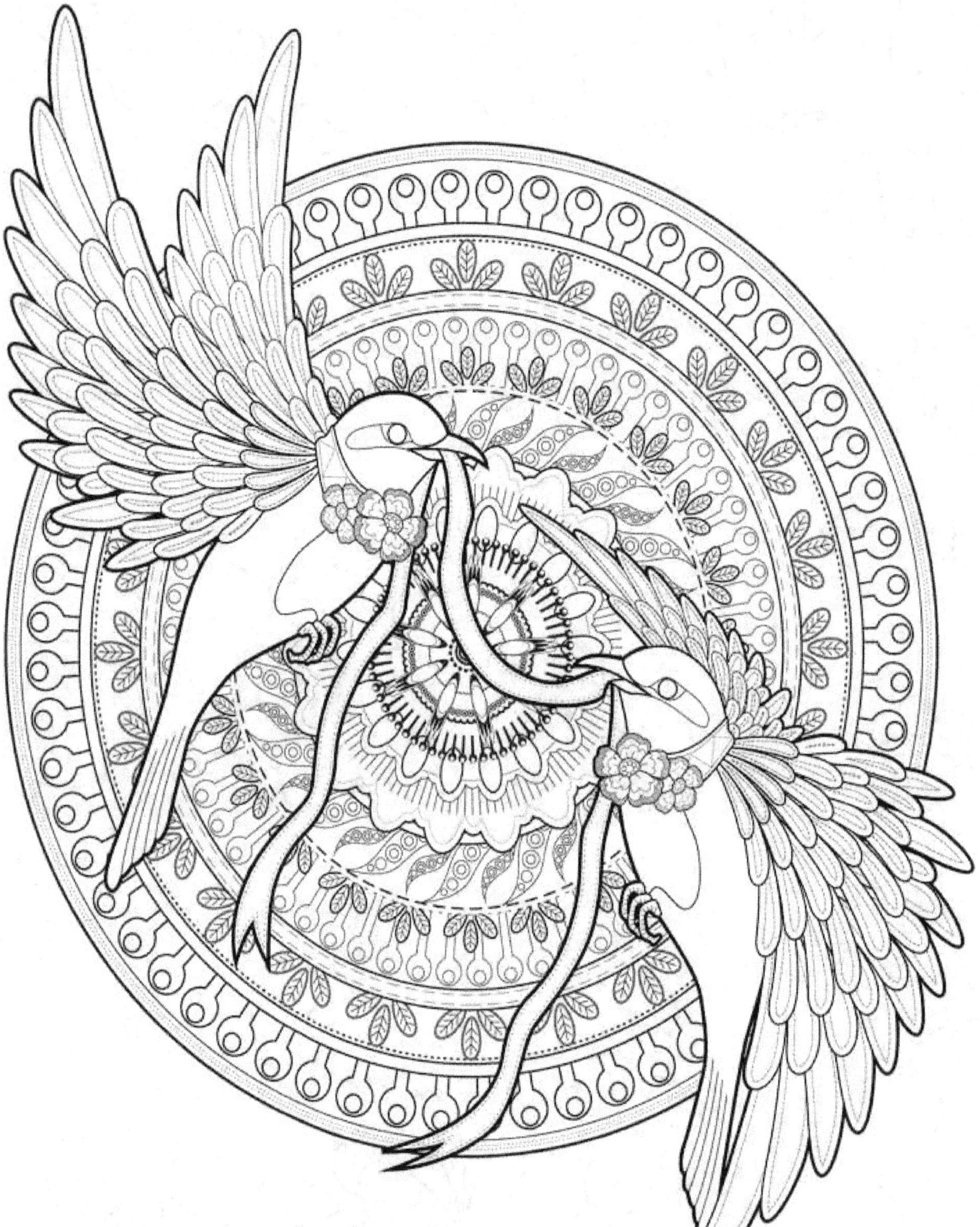

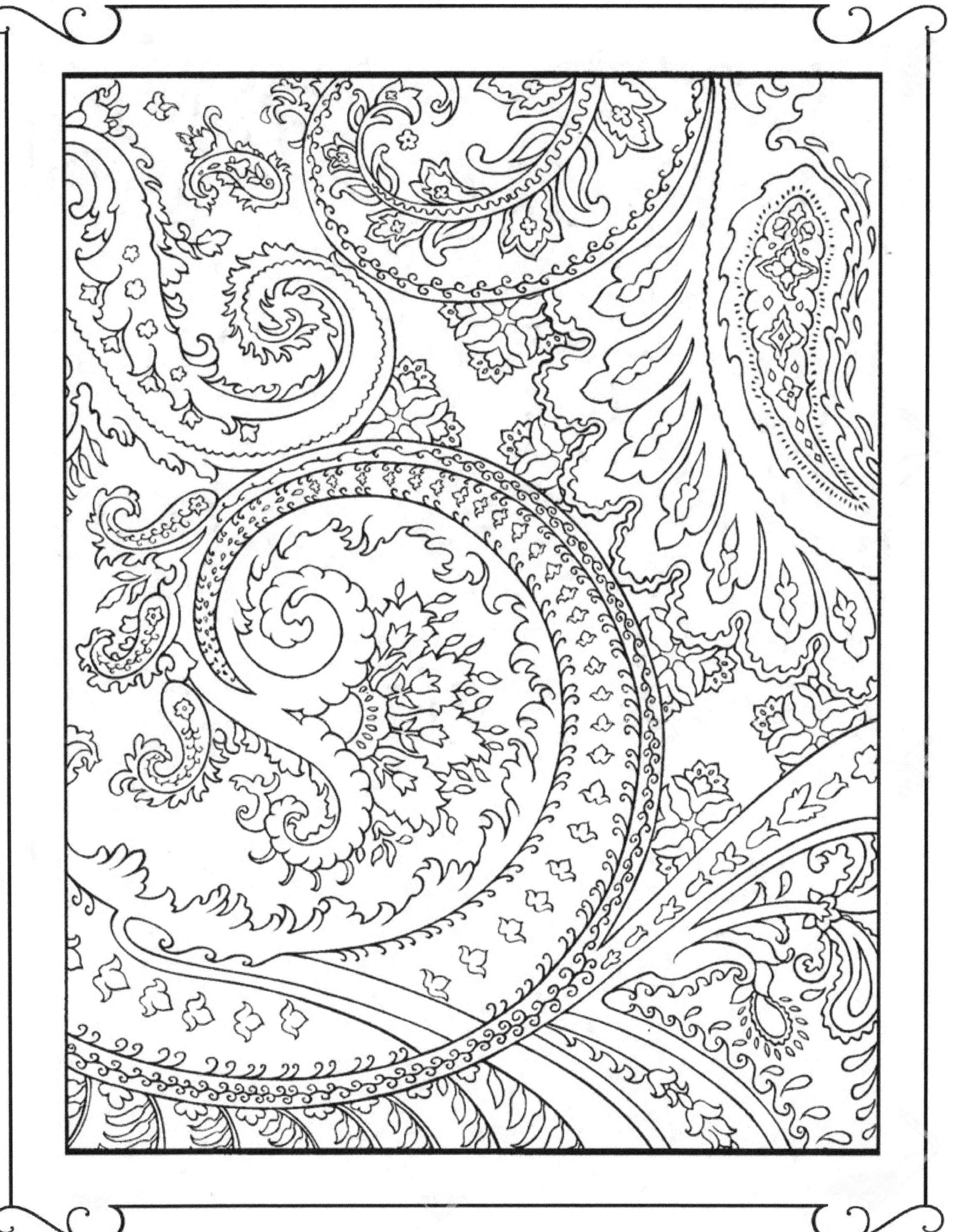

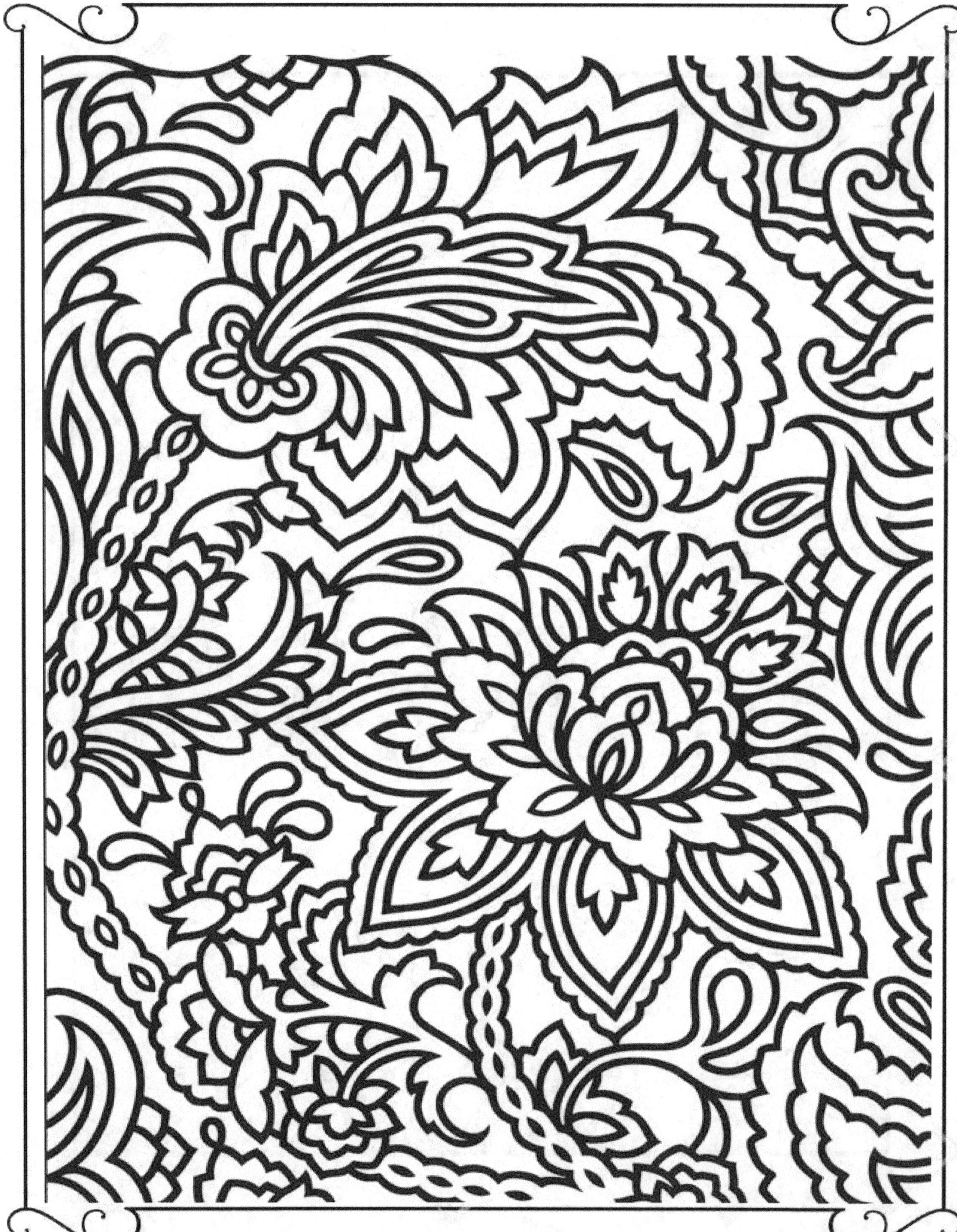

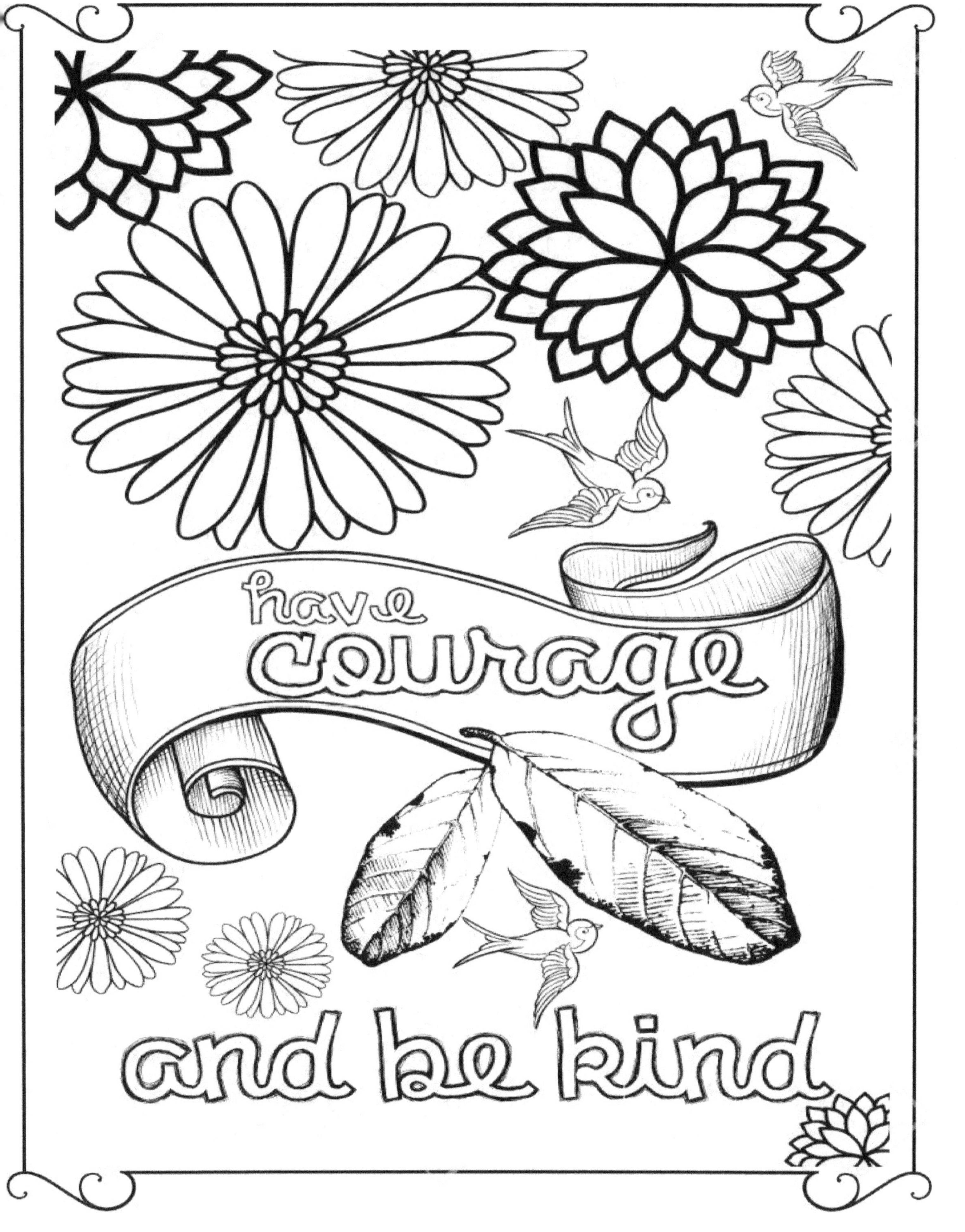
have
courage
and be kind

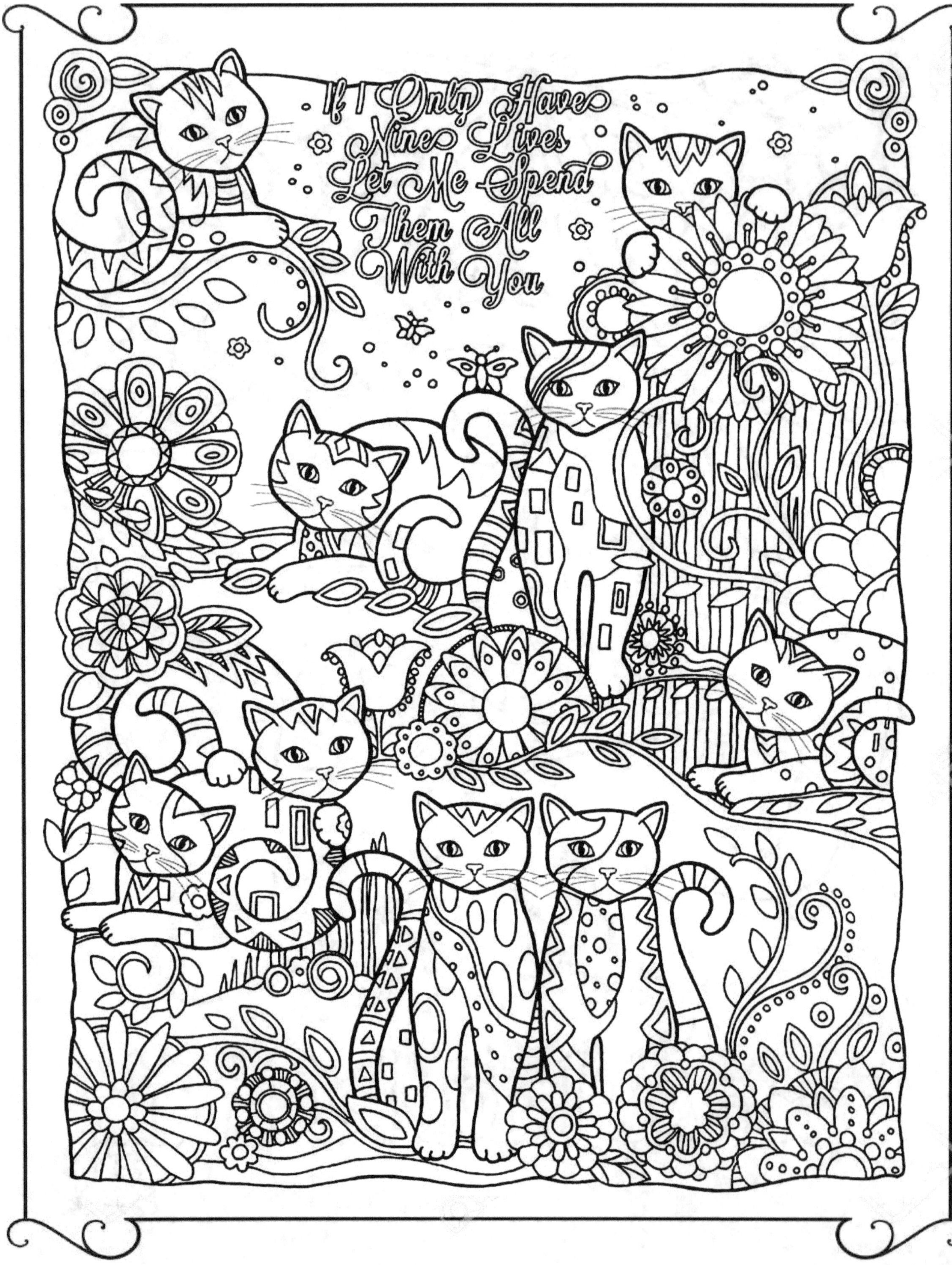
If I Only Have
Nine Lives
Let Me Spend
Them All
With You

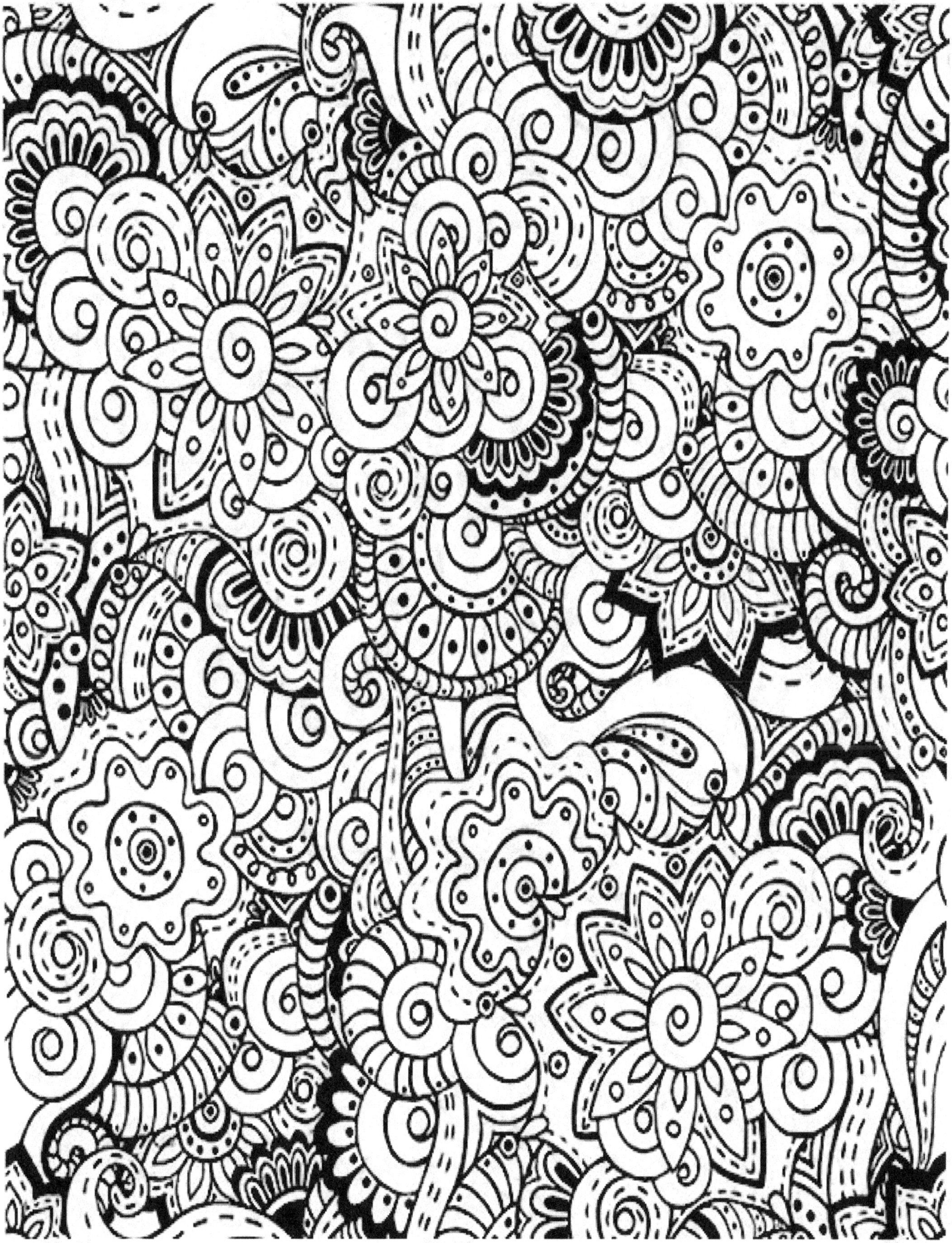

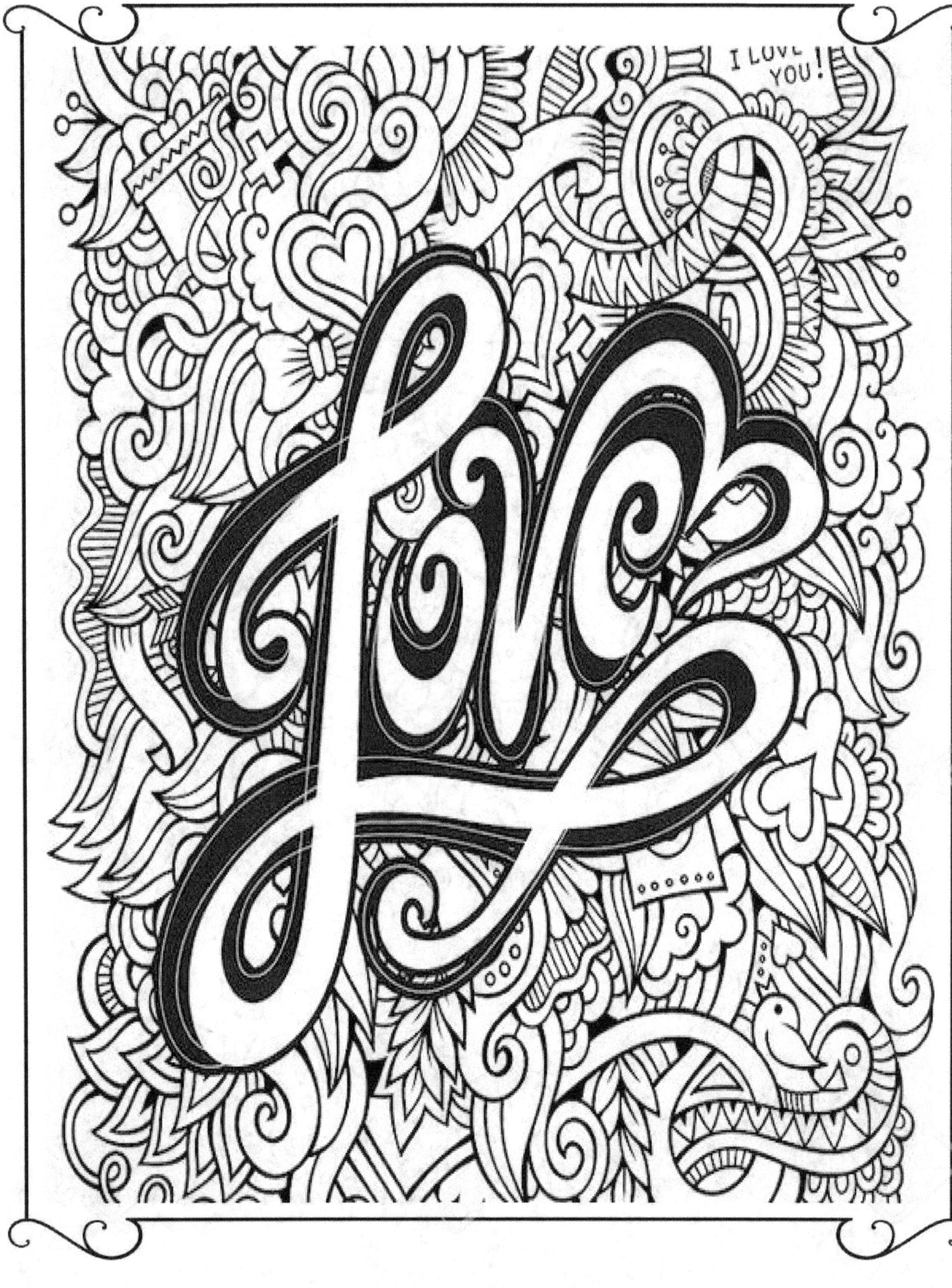
I LOVE YOU!
Love

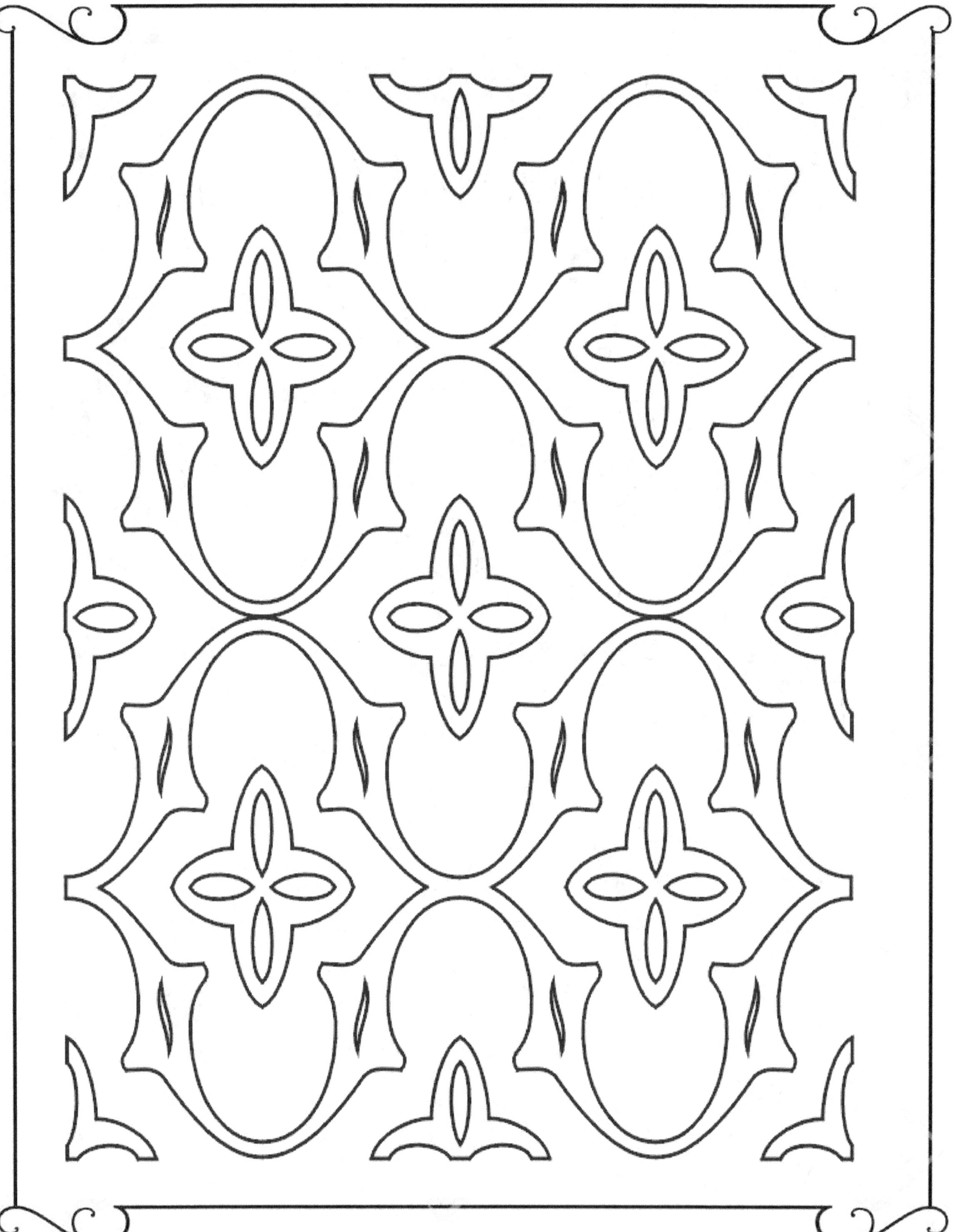

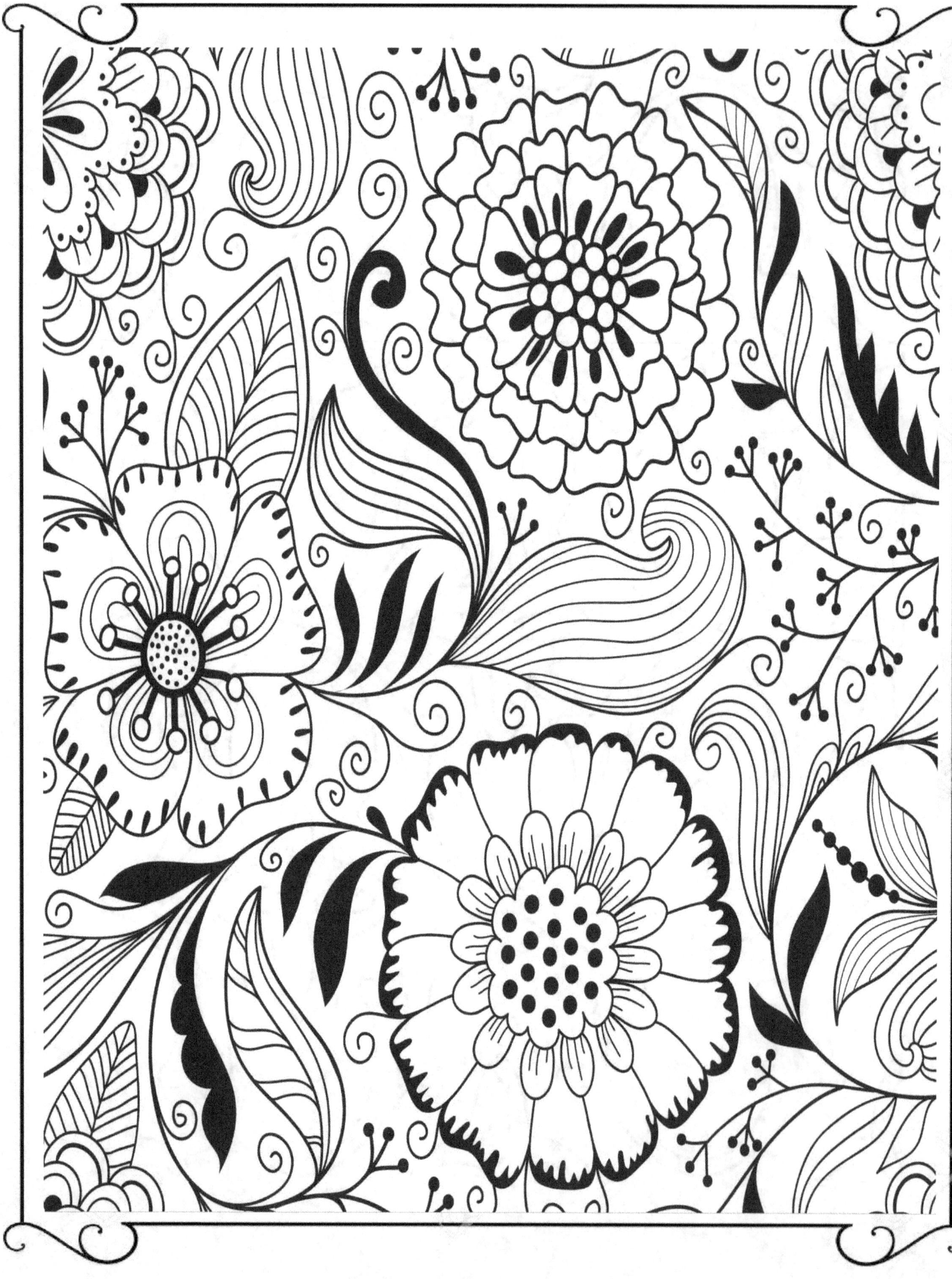

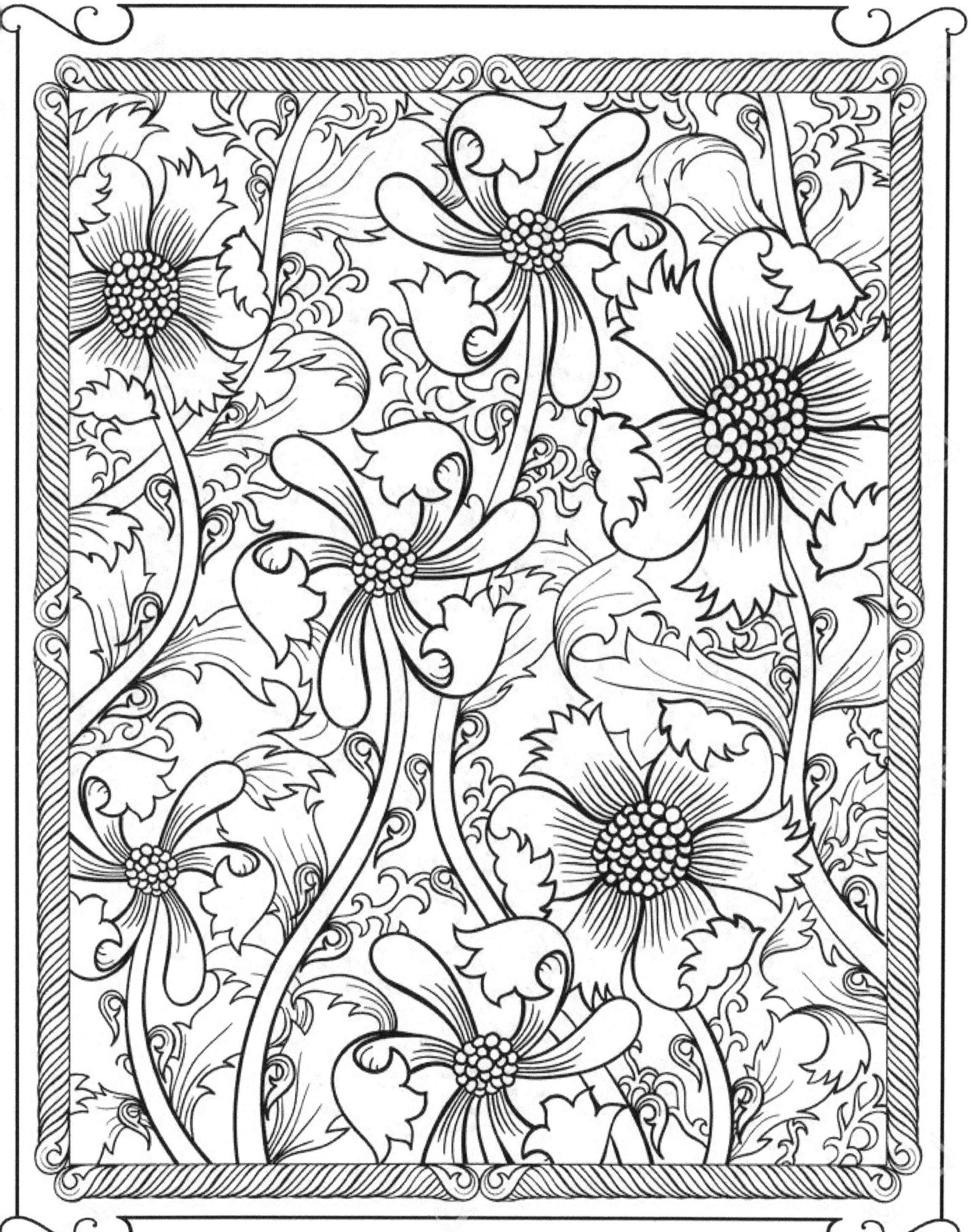

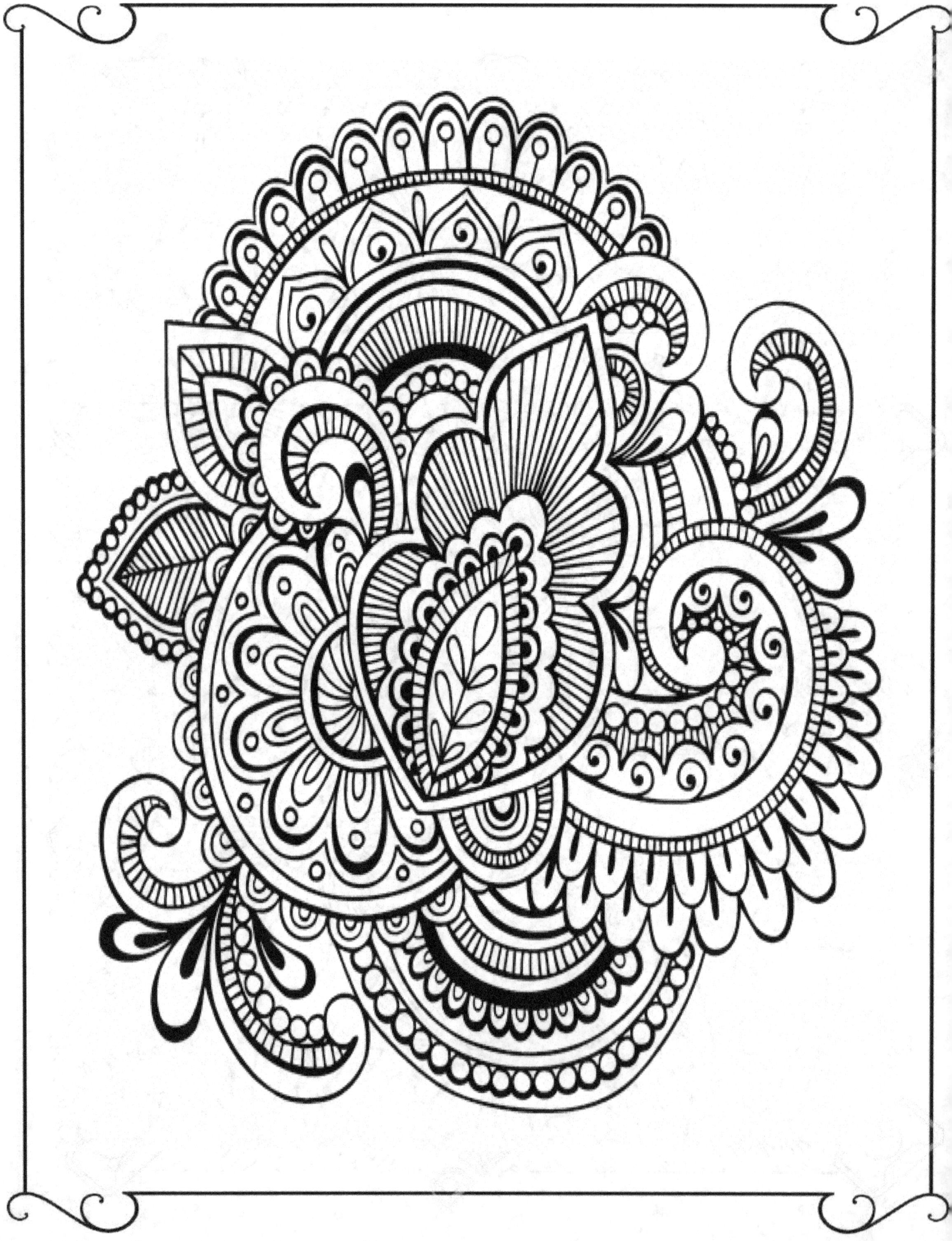

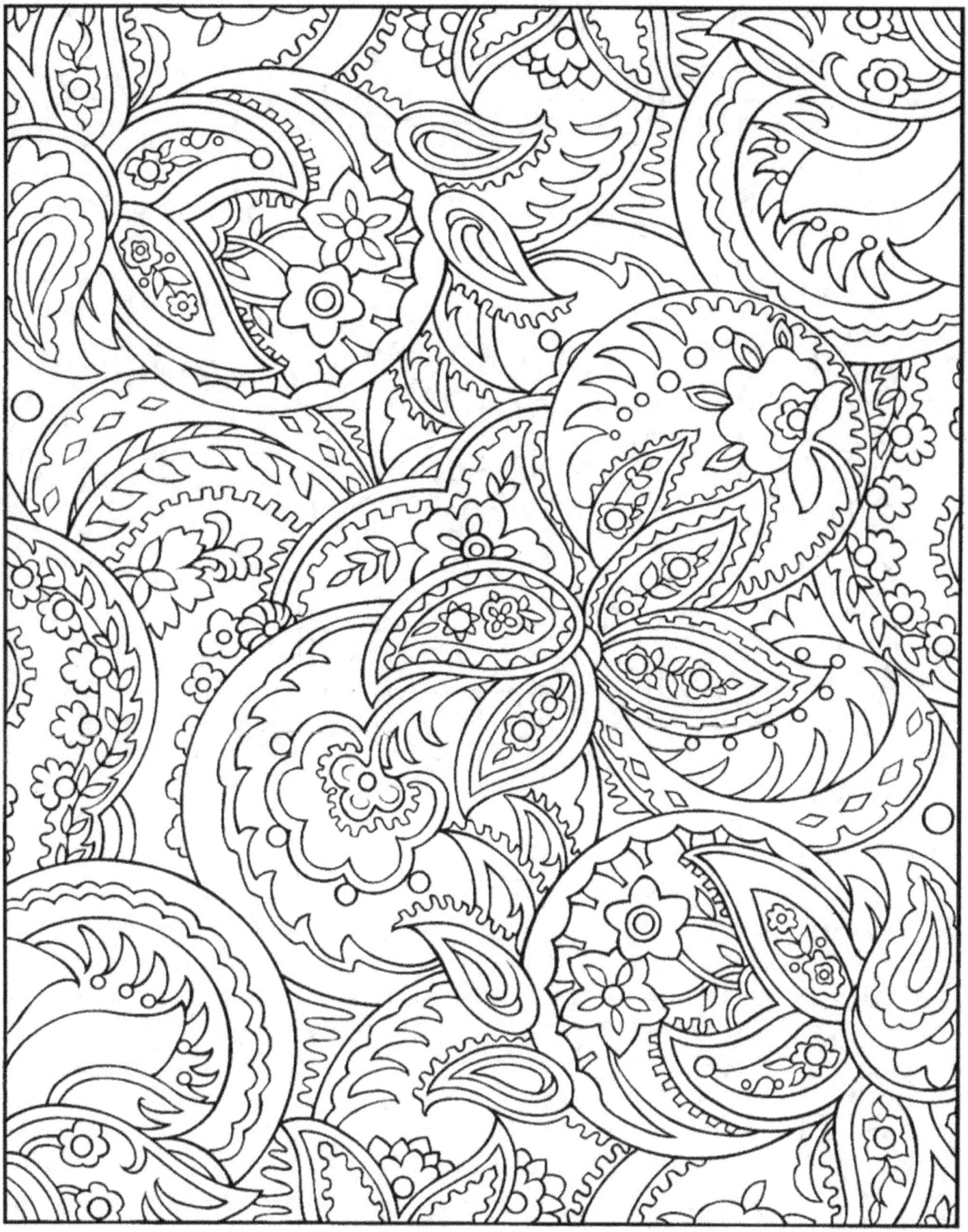

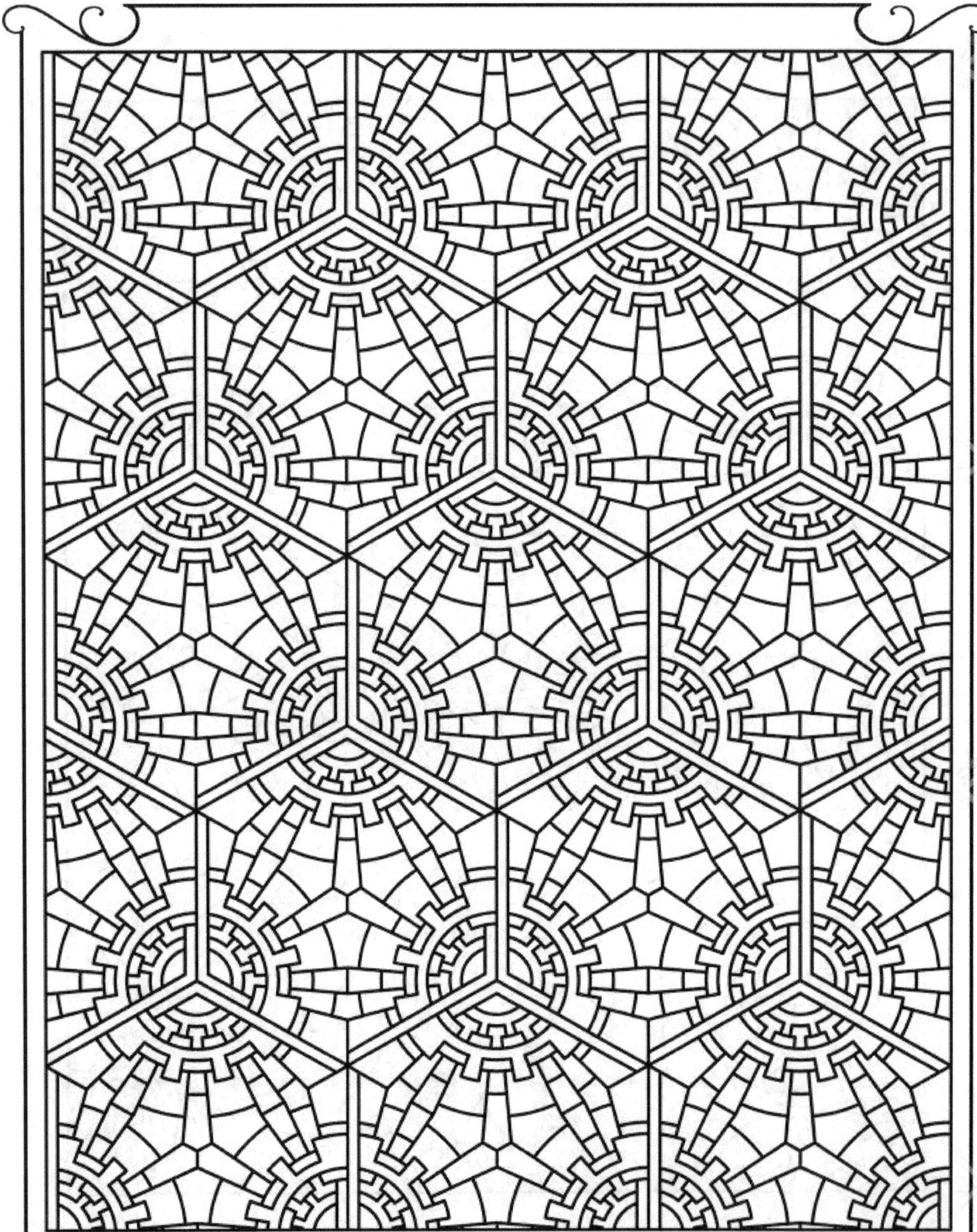

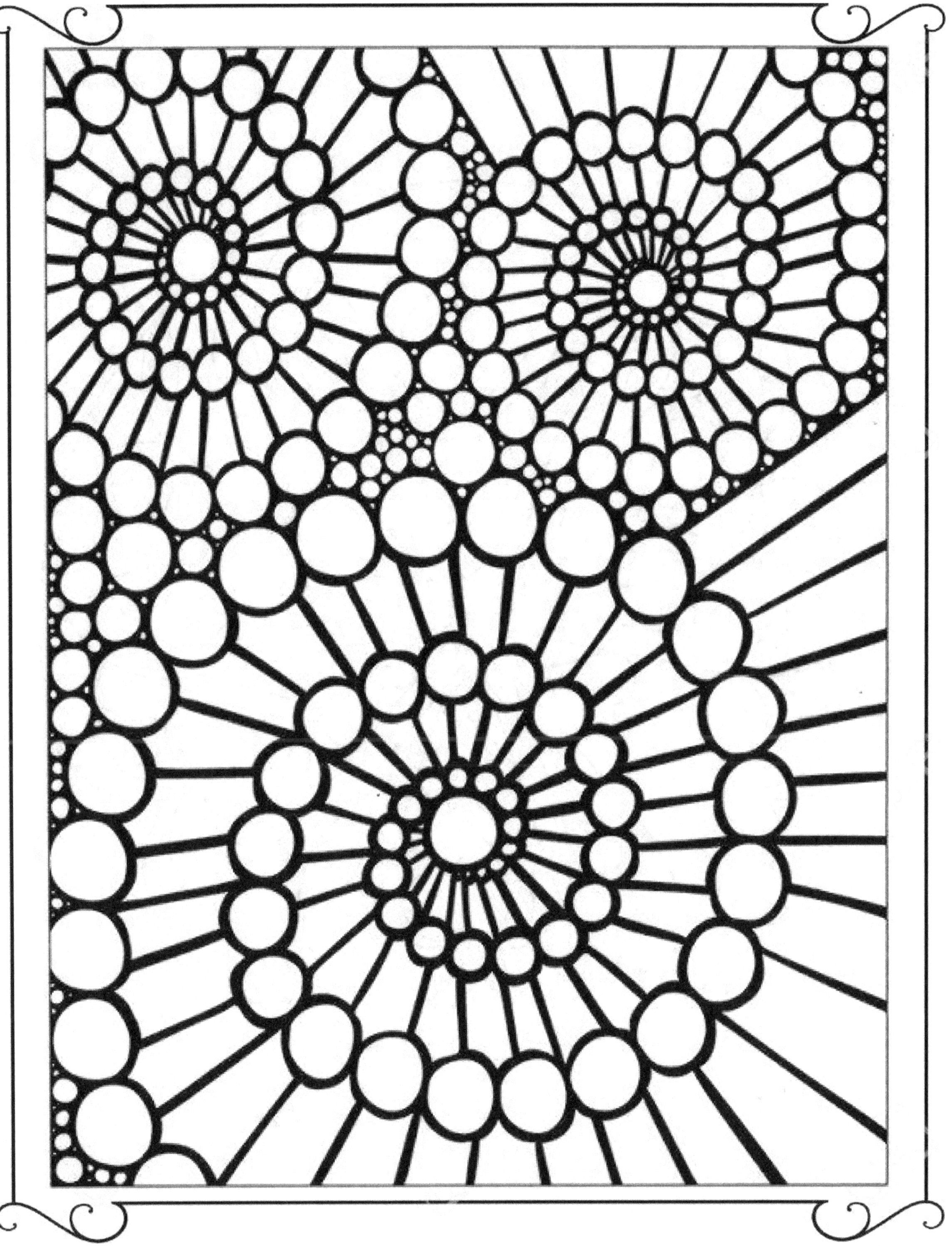

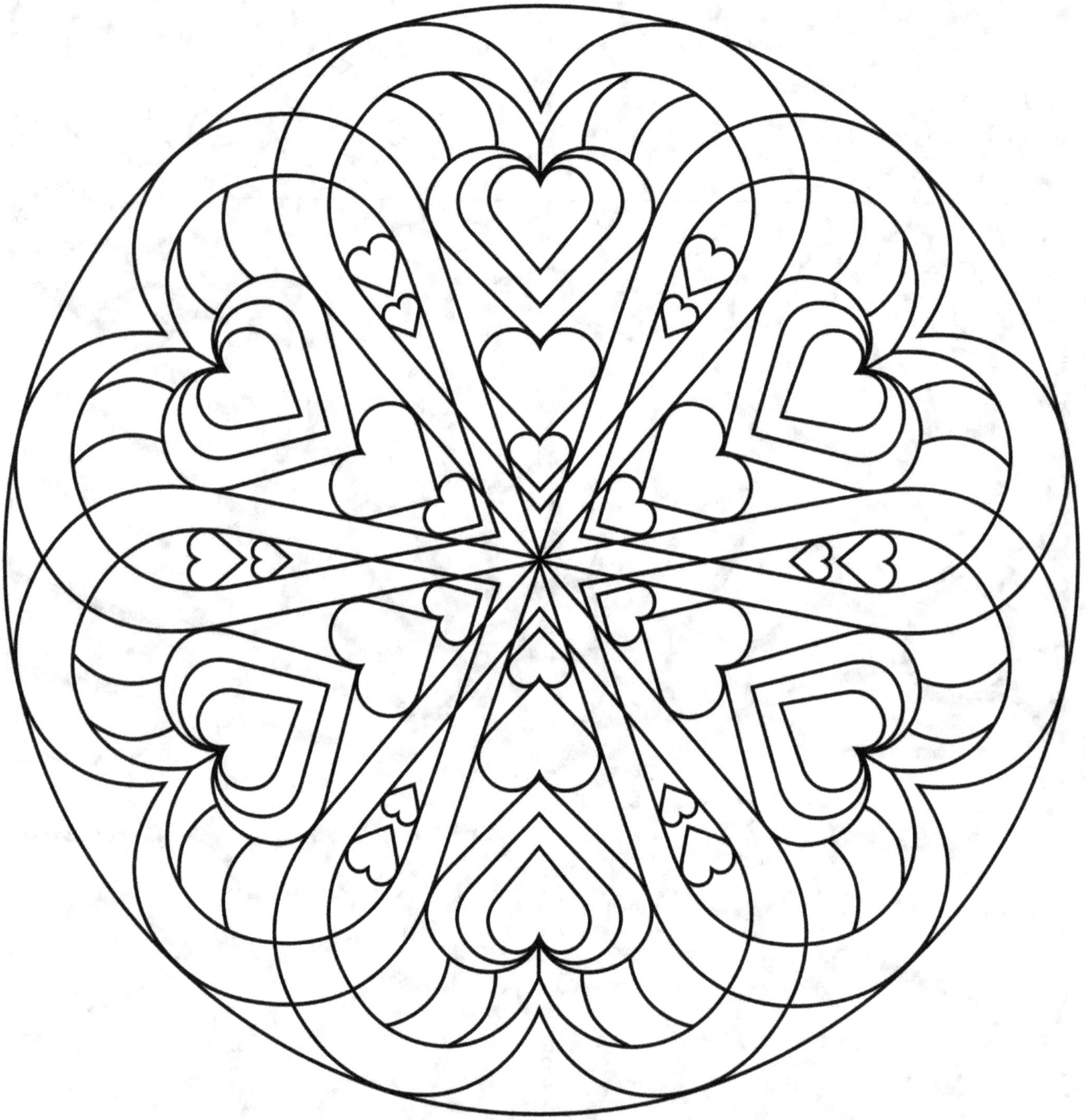

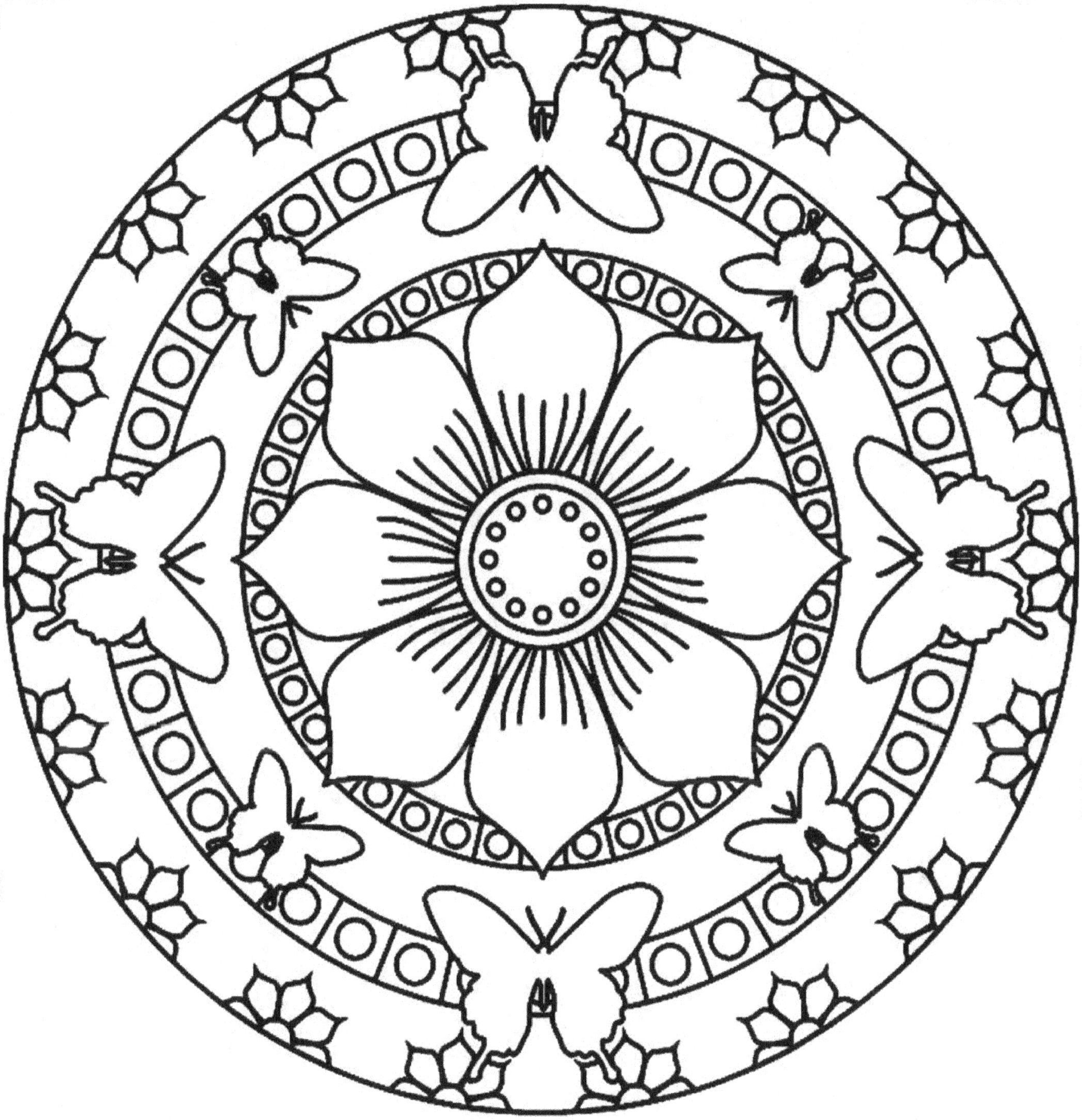

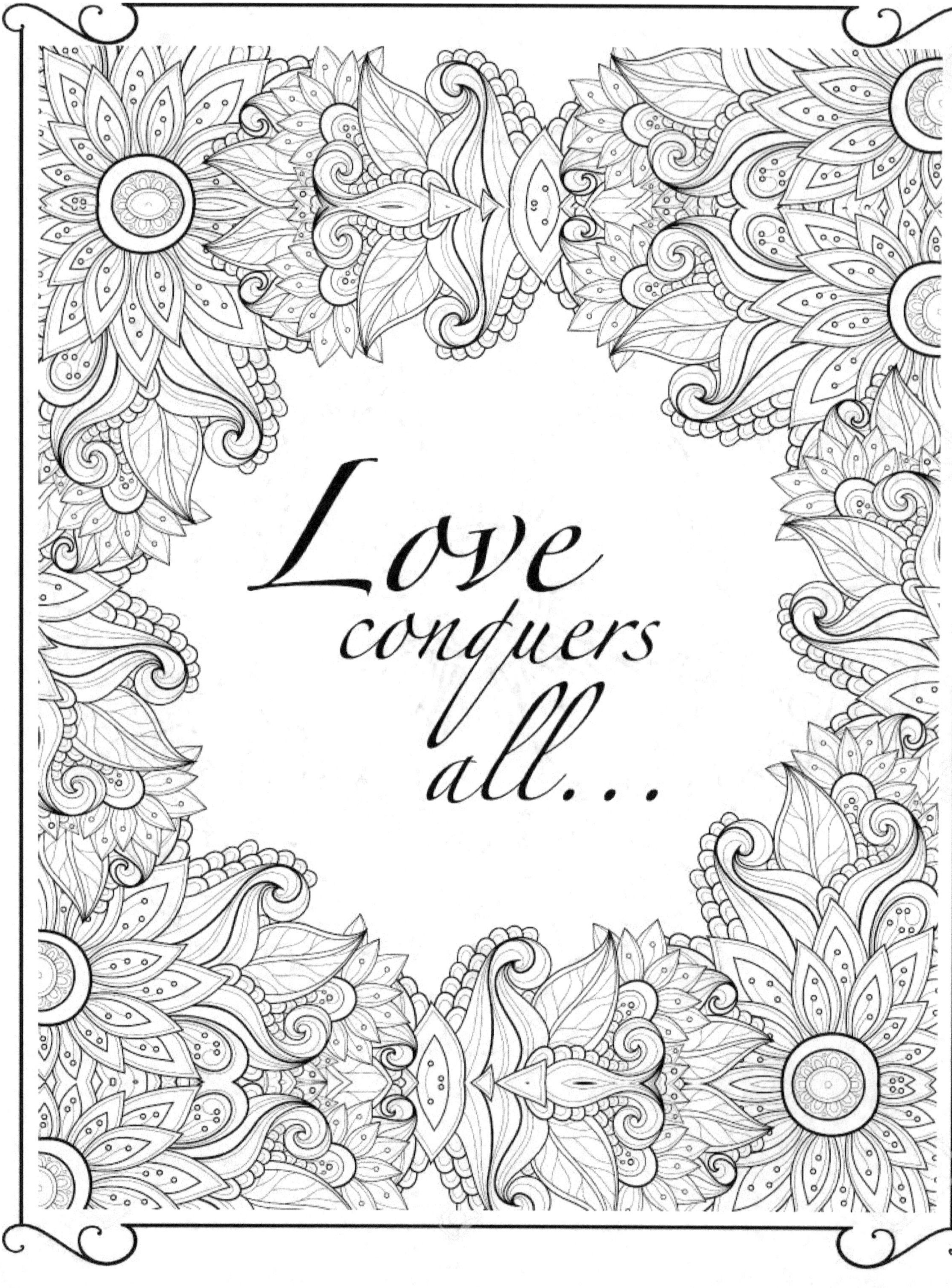
Love
conquers
all...

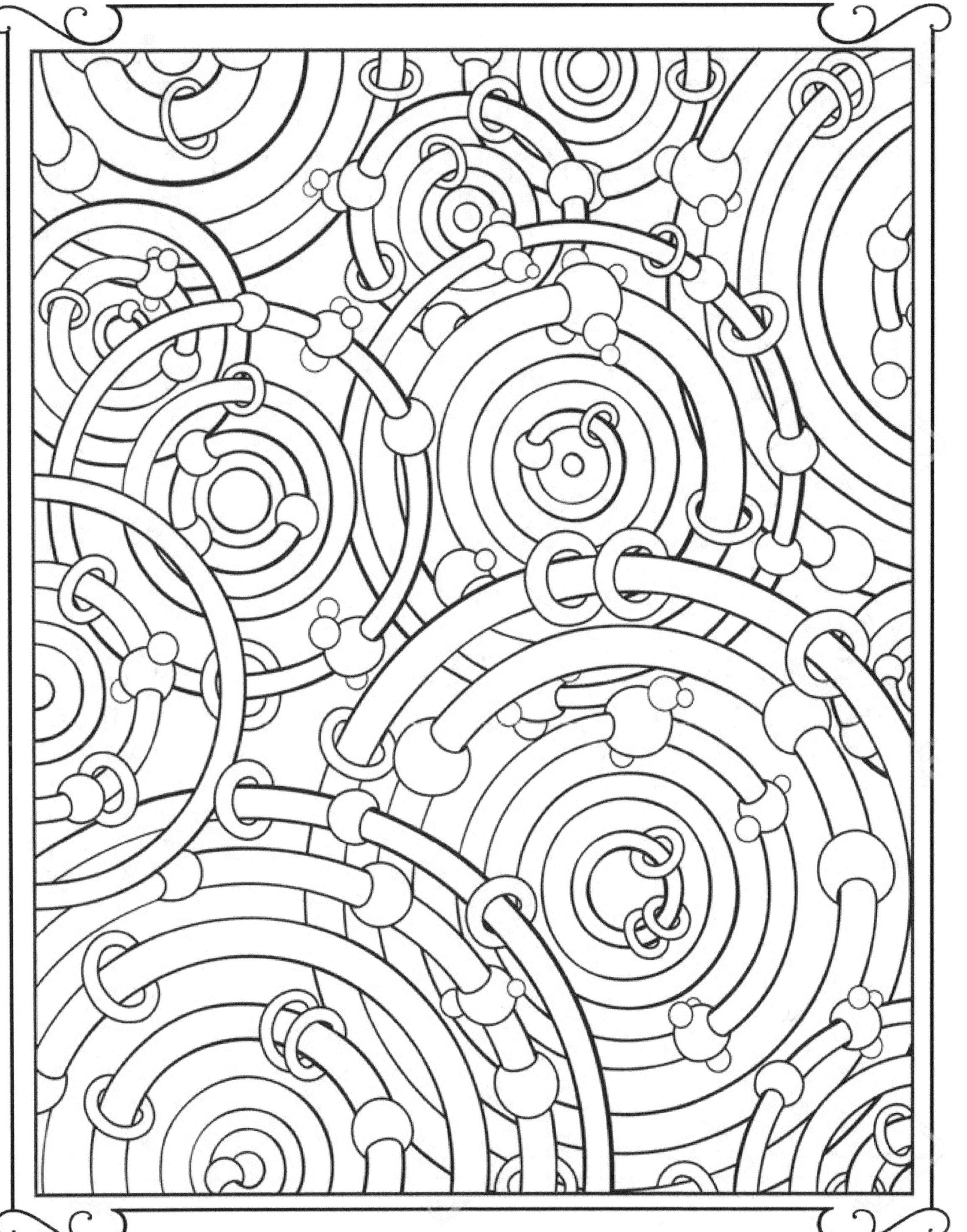

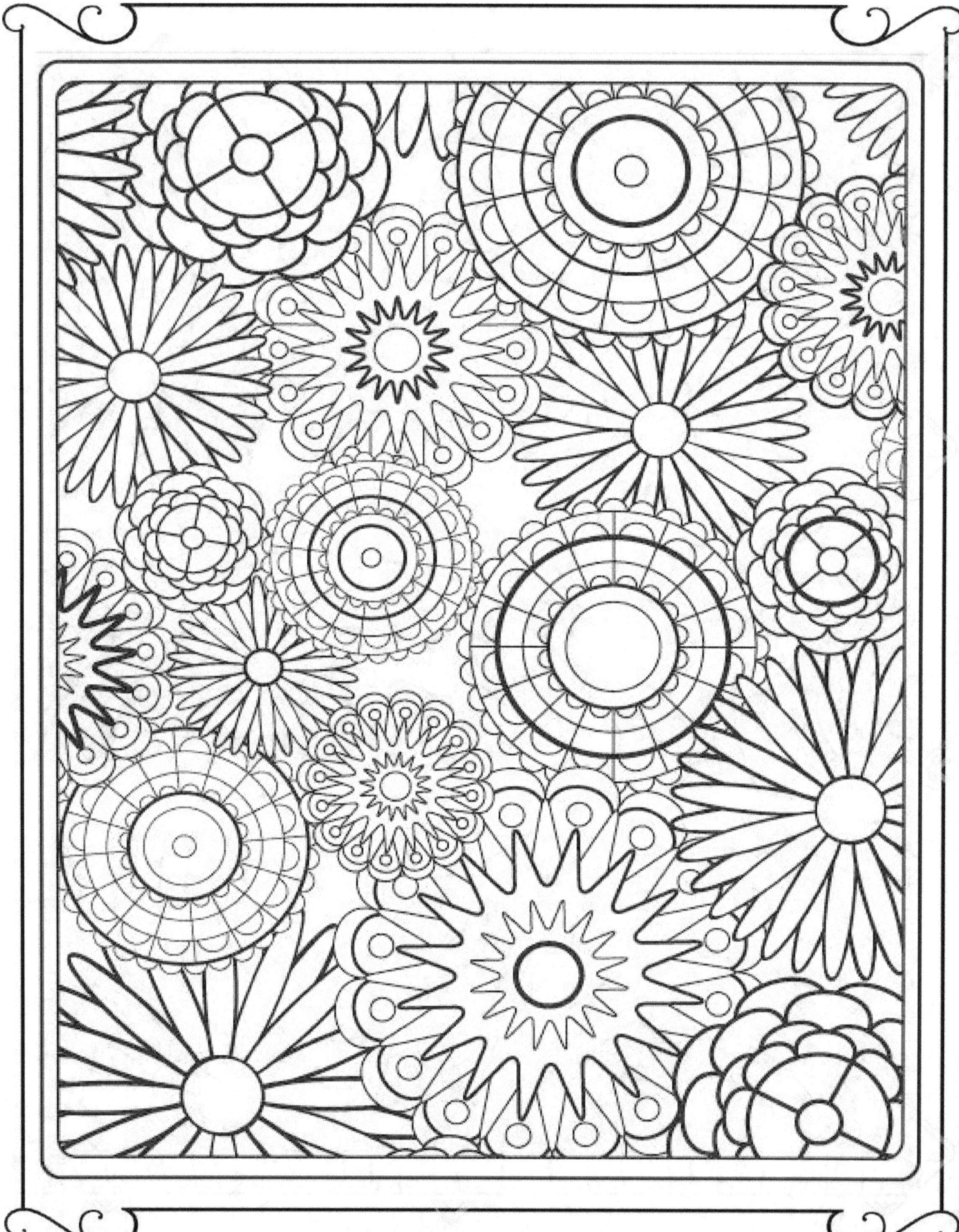

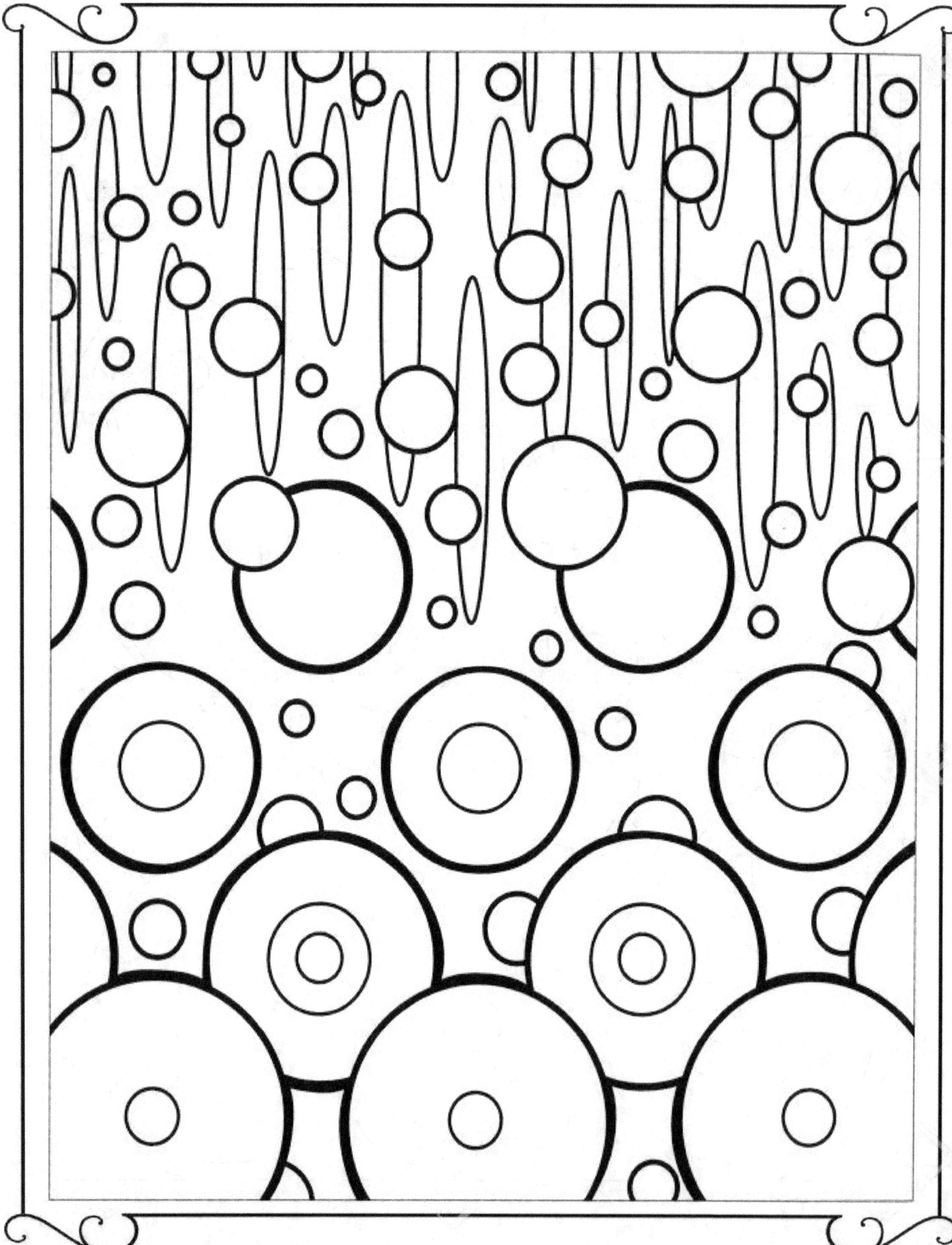

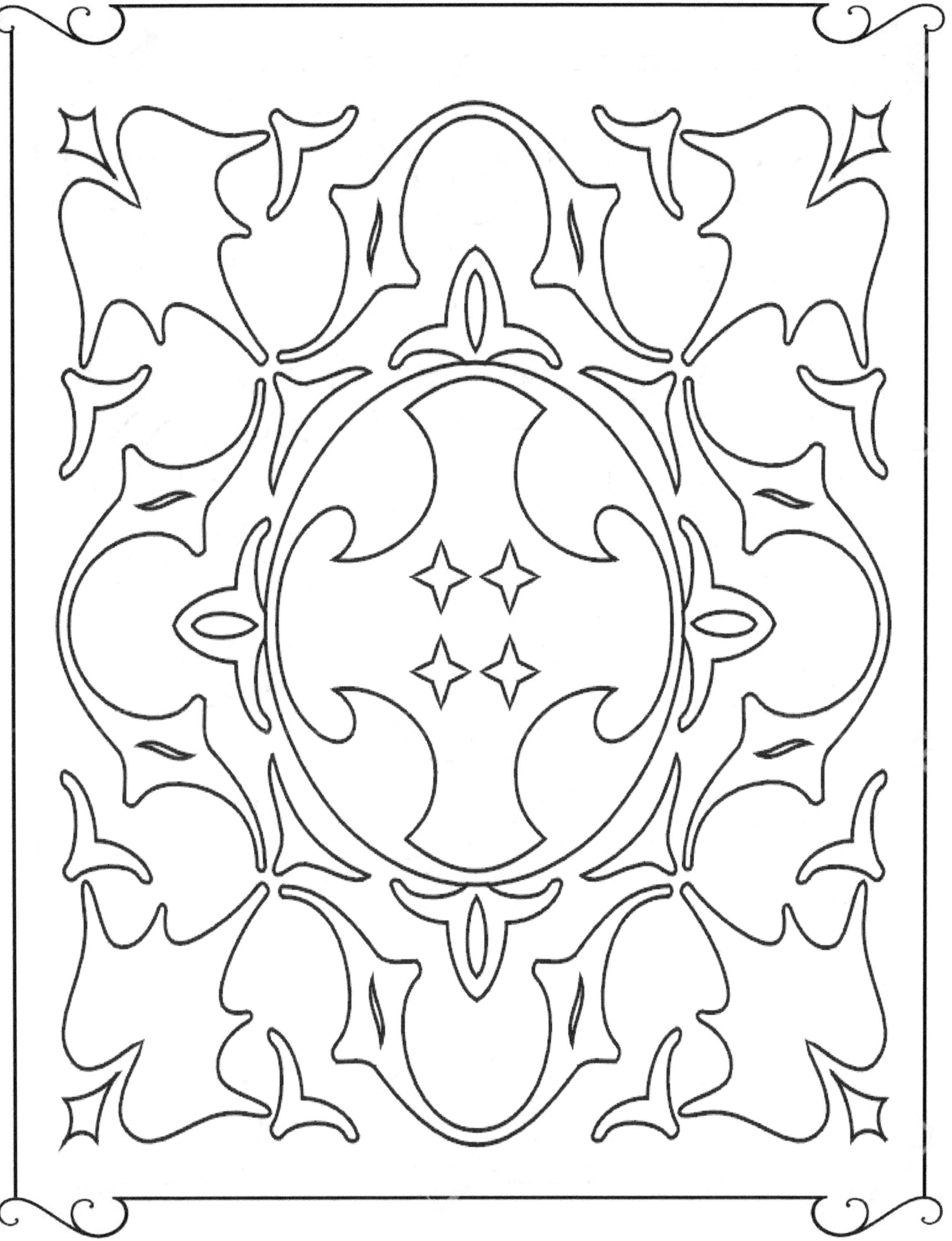

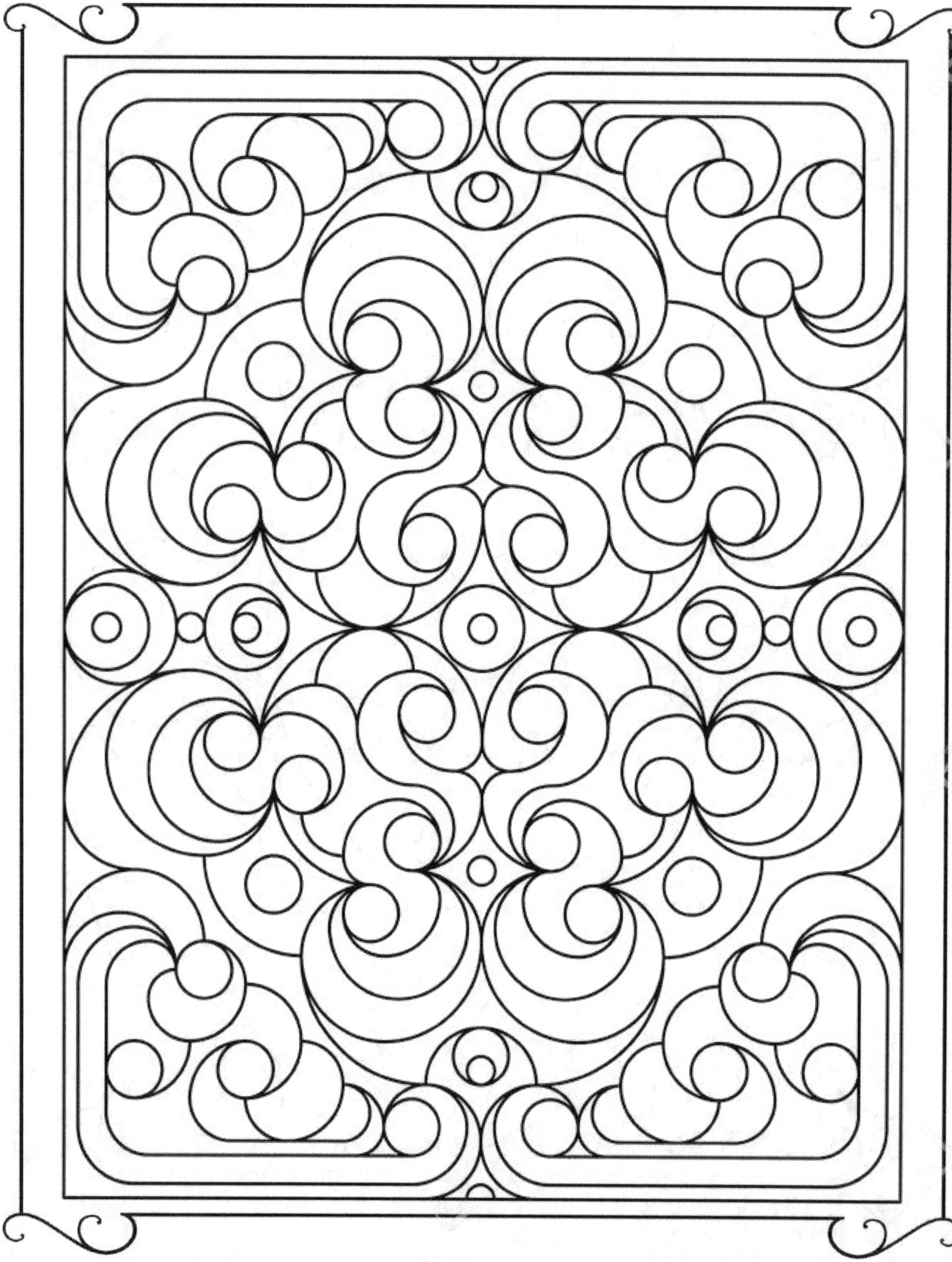

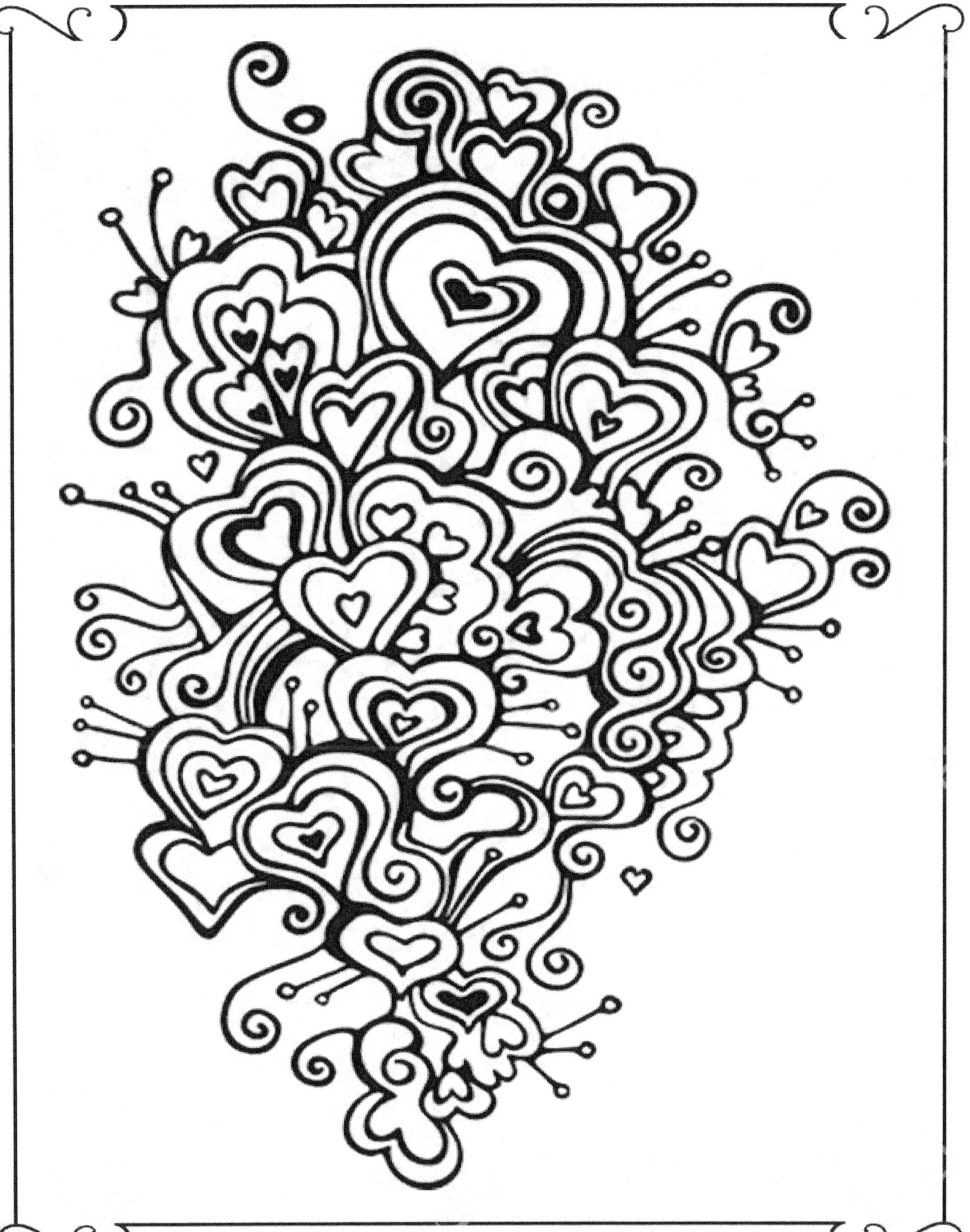

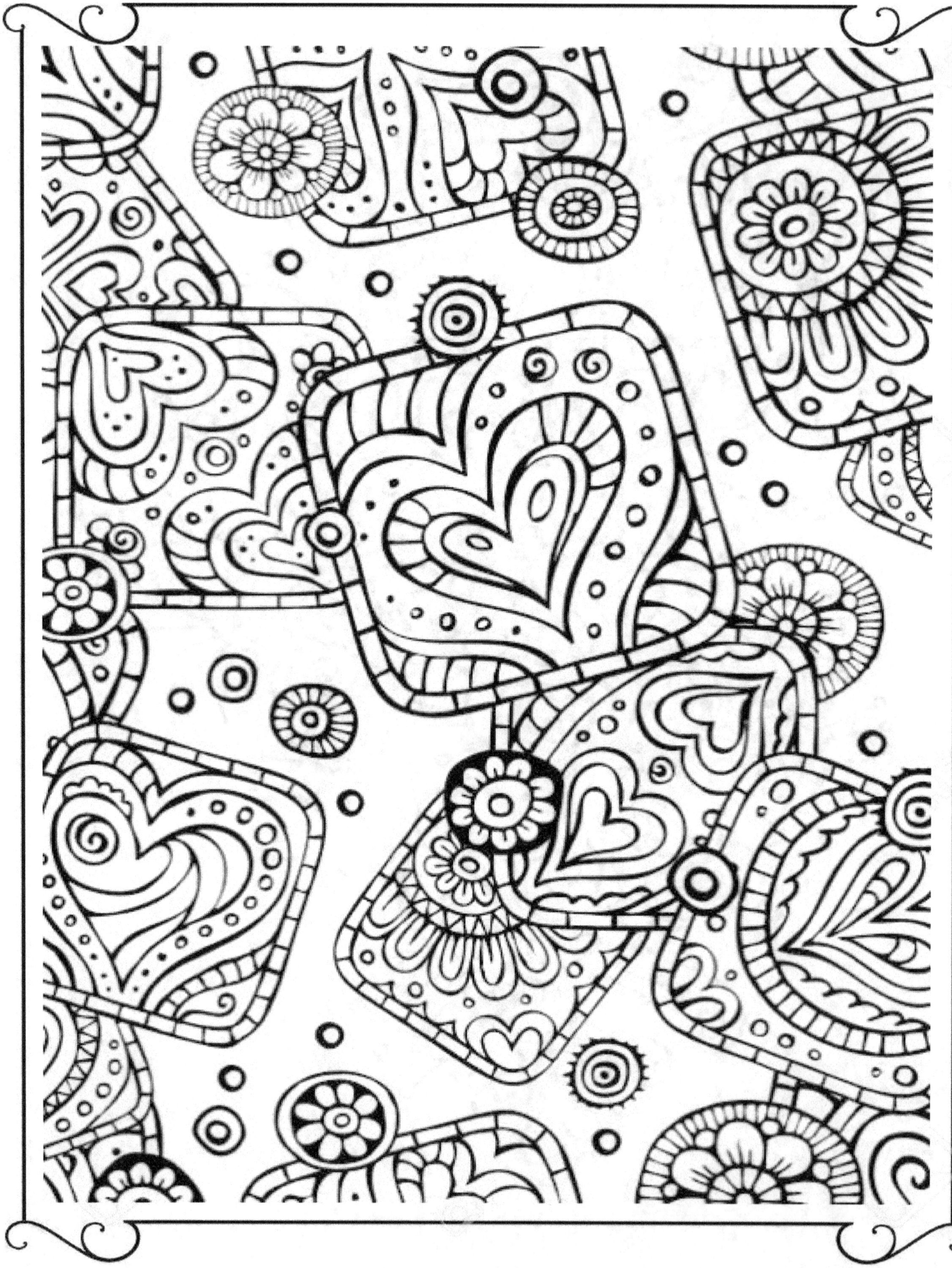

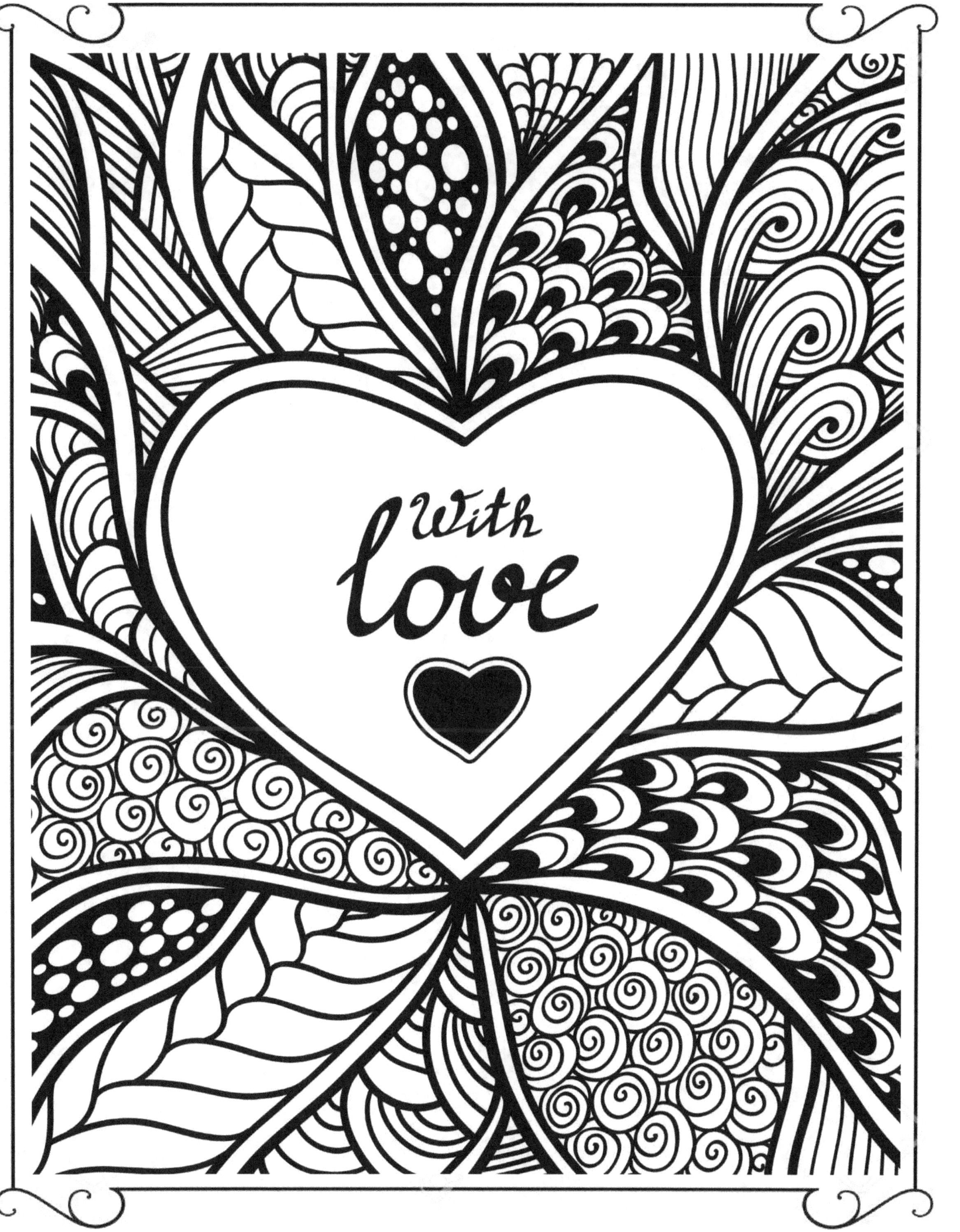
With
love

www.ingramcontent.com/pod-product-compliance
Lightning Source LLC
Chambersburg PA
CBHW080848220526
45467CB00008B/2427
* 9 7 9 8 6 8 8 3 7 5 7 2 5 *